*"Everything Within
the Revolution"*

Series in Political Economy
and Economic Development in Latin America

Series Editor
Andrew Zimbalist
Smith College

†Available in hardcover and paperback

"Everything Within the Revolution"

Cuban Strategies for Social Development Since 1960

Thomas C. Dalton

Westview Press

Boulder • San Francisco • Oxford

Series in Political Economy and Economic Development in Latin America

This Westview softcover edition is printed on acid-free paper and bound in library-quality, coated covers that carry the highest rating of the National Association of State Textbook Administrators, in consultation with the Association of American Publishers and the Book Manufacturers' Institute.

Published in 1993 in the United States of America by Westview Press, Inc., 5500 Central Avenue, Boulder, Colorado 80301-2877, and in the United Kingdom by Westview Press, 36 Lonsdale Road, Summertown, Oxford OX2 7EW

Library of Congress Cataloging-in-Publication Data
Dalton, Thomas Carlyle.
   "Everything within the revolution" : Cuban strategies for social
development since 1960 / Thomas C. Dalton.
      p.   cm. — (Series in political economy and economic
development in Latin America)
   Includes bibliographical references and index.
   ISBN 0-8133-8228-9
   1. Cuba—Social policy.   2. Cuba—Social conditions–1959–   .
3. Cuba—Economic policy.   I. Title.   II. Series.
HN203.5.D35   1993
361.6'1'097291—dc20   93-14906
                                                                        CIP

Printed and bound in the United States of America

The paper used in this publication meets the requirements
of the American National Standard for Permanence of Paper
for Printed Library Materials Z39.48-1984.

10   9   8   7   6   5   4   3   2   1

To Linda Catherine Dalton

Contents

Part 2
The Transition to New Strategies:
Institutionalization and Regulation

Part 3
The Professionalization of Prevention

Part 4
Conclusion and Assessment

Preface

This book stems from my frustration with the limitations of comparative studies of political development. Since taking a comparative politics seminar in the 1970s, I have been dissatisfied with the theory and criteria used to understand and measure the diverse processes of development in socialist states. The Cuban revolutionary experience seems to defy the straightforward application of Western or Marxist-Leninist theories of development because Cuban leaders have defined their nation's goals in terms of societal well-being. Moreover, Cuban development has been shaped by the forces of nationalism and the struggle to overcome external domination and internal doubt. The persistence of the Cuban revolution despite the collapse of communist rule in the Former Soviet Union and Eastern Europe stimulated me to examine how the Cuban approach to social development might explain this anomaly.

I owe a large debt to Andrew Zimbalist for his encouragement, thoughtful advice, and helpful criticism during every stage of the research and preparation of the book. I also would like to thank John Kirk, Marifeli Pérez-Stable, and Frank Fitzgerald for their helpful suggestions. Finally, I express my appreciation to William Ratliff of the Hoover Institution, Stanford University; Eduardo Lozano of the Center for Latin American Studies, University of Pittsburgh; and Irving Kessler of the Center for Cuban Studies, New York, for their assistance in obtaining Cuban journals and reports.

Thomas C. Dalton

Introduction

Over the past quarter century Cuba's social development strategies have changed, reflecting the different problems the regime has encountered and the priorities it has set to implement its socialist conception of political order. This analysis focuses on (1) psychological and cultural constraints to social reorganization; (2) the role that party cadres, mass organizations, and professionals have played in the implementation of social policies; (3) how their roles have changed; (4) an explanation of why strategies for social development have changed over time; and (5) an assessment of their impact on governance processes.

In the initial stages of the revolution, law was used as a tool to increase awareness of new regime norms and to generate participation through programs that mobilized citizens on behalf of educational goals, such as increased literacy. During these early years the regime also undertook a substantial redistribution of property and a reassignment of professional skills and labor to occupational roles and structures considered more socially appropriate and economically productive. These strategies of mobilization and redistribution were not sufficient by themselves, however, to harness the will and resources necessary to achieve political and economic stability. Much of their appeal depended on people's persistent feelings of injustice and the desire to achieve rapid change.

Two other strategies appeared in the 1970s to rectify a number of social and economic problems plaguing the Cuban regime. One was the adoption of a constitution in 1976 and the creation of formal institutions of governance at the national, regional, and local levels. The other involved the adoption, primarily by decree, of comprehensive criminal and civil statutes along with a myriad of administrative codes that prescribed the rights, duties, and expectations of families, children, and workers. These strategies have been much more particularistic, prescriptive, and regulatory in their scope and method than their predecessors.

One of the most significant features of the transition from strategies of *mobilization* and *redistribution* to those of *institutionalization* and *regulation* has been the increasing involvement of psychologists, psychiatrists, physicians, and other professionals in the generation and implementation of policies of social control. Government and party officials are now drawing upon medical knowledge and behavioral research to buttress their efforts to articulate norms of conduct and work befitting a socialist conception of persons. These norms then serve as standards by which productive capacity is measured and success is achieved in an occupation. Although professional expertise has not displaced the leadership role of mass organizations in social and educational policies, it has introduced a new element of competition for proximity to and leverage over policymaking processes.

A growing body of scholarly literature describes recent developments in Cuban law, politics, medicine, and society. This introduction presents conceptual and methodological issues pertinent to understanding the problems of social development within the context of comparative studies of socialist states. My subsequent analysis is presented in four parts.

Part 1 examines the conceptual underpinnings of the Cuban revolution and describes the difficulties that beset the initial attempts to use law and nonmaterial incentives to create new men and women under socialism. Chapter 1 traces the origins of *conciencia* (the ethic of sacrifice) and *lucha* (struggle) in order to clarify the scope of revolutionary transformation that Fidel Castro and Che Guevara envisioned. The Cuban revolution has exhibited a remarkable continuity in the pursuit of ideals enunciated by Guevara and Castro despite numerous setbacks and increased challenges voiced by critics and skepticism among observers. I also examine the principles that the *guerrilla foco* yielded to guide subsequent processes of social reconstruction and to structure Cuba's relationship with the Soviet Union and internationalist policies in the Third World. Chapter 2 describes the attempt to use mechanisms of popular justice to build support for policies to redistribute wealth and ration goods and services. I examine the difficulties that the Committees for the Defense of the Revolution (CDRs) faced in reconciling the dual roles they assumed in controlling the distribution of goods while administering the system of people's justice, and I describe the circumstances that led to the reassignment of the CDRs to crime-prevention activities. This experiment in judicial reform was followed by a strategy designed to reorganize the workplace and subject Cuban workers to new standards by which their performance could be measured and disciplined. Chapter 3 describes how moral incentives were used to reorganize work and wage structures; examines the role that the party, workers, unions, management, and the Women's Federation (FMC) have played in this process; and explores the dilemma of productivity versus workers' rights posed by the adoption and expansion of alternative structures of labor.

In Part 2 I examine why new strategies were being considered at the end of the 1960s that could provide stable forms of governance and bring about the most effective conservation and utilization of human resources. Thus, Chapter 4 explores factors contributing to a transition to strategies involving the strengthening of families and child-rearing practices and the prevention of delinquency. I also describe the theories and experimental group studies psychologists have employed to derive norms of conduct appropriate to a socialist society. Finally, I look at how social scientists explain the problem of illegal networks and corruption, and I explore the underlying relationship between dissidence and official scandals such as the Ochoa trial in 1989. Chapter 5 covers the role that formal institutions of governance, such as the national and local assemblies, the Council of State, the Politburo, and the party apparatus, play within a policymaking and implementation process that has evolved to integrate knowledge and professional judgment through continual experimentation and adjustment. I also look at recent criticisms of delegate representation and at proposals to strengthen their role in policymaking processes.

Next, Part 3 illustrates how strategies of regulation and prevention have increased the role that professionals play in policymaking and implementation. Castro increasingly relies on behavioral and survey research to obtain more accurate information about the health status and behavior of Cubans. Chapter 6 describes how psychologists have dealt with weak social ties and inadequate personal integration by articulating a conception of well-being and preventive health care that goes well beyond traditional methods of medical practice. Castro has also introduced an ambitious health care delivery program that overcomes some of the most significant organizational and professional constraints undermining previous efforts. I describe the evolution of the Cuban health-care system in Chapter 7 and examine how Cuba's massive investment in biomedical research complements the country's internationalist missions abroad while providing the justification needed to greatly enlarge mechanisms for social intervention at home.

Finally, in Part 4, I put Cuban strategies of social development in a comparative analytical perspective that enables us to generalize about the processes that Cuba has undergone in realizing its objectives of social reconstruction. This analysis explains why Cuban strategies of social development have become intertwined with Cuba's foreign policy objectives and why the strategies and techniques have changed over time; the analysis also examines how issue networks have emerged to provide professionals increased leverage over policies governed by cadre-dominated clientism and informal exchange networks. In addition, I assess Cuba's prospects for overcoming the economic difficulties, political constraints, and social resistance that continue to block the path to complete social reconstruction.

Understanding Development in Socialist Regimes

Almond and Verba's (1965) study of the elements that contribute to the development of "civic culture" remains a classic in the literature on comparative politics. The authors made a pioneering attempt to define political culture in dynamic and behavioral terms such that studies of political development could become explanatory, rather than merely descriptive, enterprises. Since that landmark work, however, the ethnocentric assumptions underpinning development and its relationship to ambiguous conceptions of "modernity" and "postmodernity" have undergone extensive criticism (Almond 1989; Wiarda 1991). Western development has not led, as it was predicted (Chilcote 1991), to the diffusion of technology and to the eradication of illiteracy, poverty, and disease throughout the developing world. Countries just attaining a modest industrial base must now compete in a new international economic order predicated on advanced technologies that require an enormous investment in basic scientific research and development.

Critics also charge that processes of economic and social development in developed, dependent, and socialist countries alike fail to conform either to Marxist-Leninist theories of the collapse of capitalism and spread of world communism or to the unilinear sequence predicted by Western theories of development in which industrialization and technological change eventuate in attitudes and behavior that contribute to social stability and political competence (Brown and Gray 1977; Cardoso and Falleto 1979; Wiatr 1989). Few scholars anticipated the depth and seriousness of the economic and social crisis that would bring about the unexpected collapse of so-called developed communist regimes in Eastern Europe and the Soviet Union. Fewer still understood the important role that ethnic and cultural forces could play in challenging the political legitimacy of communist rule. Bureaucratic authoritarianism still holds a strong grip in Latin America and in other Third World regimes, and the cycle of corruption, reform, and retrenchment continues to block radical transformations in social and occupational structures (Martz 1991; Theobald 1990). Nevertheless, Unger (1987:275–77, 324–26) persuasively argues that the sequence by which capitalist and socialist development evolves cannot be predicted in advance because these regimes are subject to forces that "destabilize" routines, resulting in strategic relationships whose outcome cannot be foreseen. According to Unger, socialist states need not be trapped in the cyclical swing between decentralization and recentralization because this cycle of reform and retrenchment is rooted in habitual reactions subject to revision under new contingencies.

One of the most perplexing issues in comparative politics is how a nation's social values and political processes are integrated to form stable and persistent patterns of institutional behavior. For example, Huntington (1981) contends that the American "creedal politics," which is predicated on social values (i.e., equality and individual rights), is characterized by a cyclical swing between moral reformism/rising expectations and cynicism/retrenchment. Similarly, the frequency of reform measures instituted in China and in other former communist regimes has led some observers to characterize them as "cycles of dissatisfaction," typified by the continuing piling up of new problems on older ones that remain unresolved (Lampton 1987:8).

The history of Latin American and Caribbean politics has conformed to a similar cycle. For example, the caudillo (leader) who blends strength with compassion and a sense of social justice has served for over a century as the ideal of effective leadership in Cuba as well as in most Latin American countries. Leaders supporting political modernization in Latin America have frequently failed to carry forward an agenda of social reform primarily because of their inability to effectively consolidate state power to rectify inequities in the distribution of wealth and social services. Corporatist structures characteristic of Latin American politics consist of complex networks of family-related economic ties that effectively block redistributive policies (Roett 1984). The momentum for reform is soon eclipsed by cynicism and the resumption of military rule. Consequently, effective change has put a premium on authority and compromise, sometimes at the expense of representativeness.

In this book, I do not equate development with modernity or underdevelopment with a backward society because competing cultural orientations may coexist even though divided by invisible barriers of space and time (Gusfield 1967; Portes 1973). Instead, I use the term *development* to refer to the processes by which national resources (both physical and human) are combined to attain technological change and economic growth, social cohesion and cultural continuity, legitimate and stable mechanisms of political governance, and recognition of a country as an equal and valued participant in the world economy. A strong technical and economic capacity alone is not sufficient by contemporary standards to sustain participation in the world economy. Countries are increasingly judged on their protection of human rights, respect for the environment, availability of hard currency, and ability to avoid costly deficits in the balance of trade.

A nation embarked on a course of development must also advance and inculcate certain beliefs about the origin and basis of national identity, specify and continually redefine national objectives and the strategies for their attainment, and be capable of mobilizing the will and support of the majority in overcoming constraints to development. Third World countries undergoing convulsive change in the transition from colonial rule or intervention face much greater hardship and uncertainty in confronting these tasks than do Western societies whose ideas about authority, rights, and the scope and limits of governmental intervention have had time to evolve. Consequently, as Donnelly (1989:312–13) points out, pressures for social equity and redistribution inevitably involve some degree of conflict and repression in the early stages of development, especially in states attempting to overcome a tradition of authoritarian and corrupt regimes.

The conventional yardstick by which development has been measured is productivity and national economic growth. Although an important indicator, economic performance alone reveals little about the quality of a nation's social infrastructure. For example, South Africa under apartheid and the Philippines under Ferdinand Marcos performed well economically amidst political injustice and gross social inequities. Indicators of social development such as literacy, health, employment, and rights serve as measures of progress in terms of individual autonomy, development, and advancement. By *social* development I mean the creation of institutions and services that provide for the growth, education, health, welfare, safety, and privacy of individuals and families; that generate learning opportunities for the development of judgment; that enable the acquisition of technical competence for advancement in one's chosen occupation; and that provide avenues for self-expression, participation, and leadership in civic culture as well as in policymaking and governance processes.

One of the most important factors bearing on social development is the capacity to acquire knowledge and the techniques necessary to confront the dual demands for economic performance and social betterment. This is precisely the point at which the availability of professional expertise becomes crucial to the strategies a regime selects to achieve its goals. Social knowledge is rarely developed in the abstract; it is organized through particular methods of inquiry that generate specific *techniques* with which to solve socially significant problems. Experimentation has become a favored technique in Cuban and U.S. regimes alike to generate as well as to apply knowledge for social problem solving. Experimentation provides a way to determine the consequences of factors introduced into situations fraught with uncertainty before committing the government to endorsement or implementation on a broader scale.

In Cuba, policies for social development are derived from a continual learning cycle of experimentation, implementation, and adjustment. Mass organizations such as the FMC and the CDRs play an important role in ensuring that the provinces achieve equity, uniformity, and conformity in handling problems of health, crime, and delinquency in their communities. This approach has increased popular support for these policies, but it has also greatly enlarged the role of professional experts in the processes of social development. Thus, party cadres, professionals, and scientists now share pivotal but uncertain roles in reconciling potential policy conflicts between national and local governmental and administrative control. The integrity and credibility of social scientists and medical professionals are clearly at the heart of this dilemma.

At present, we are gradually learning how citizens have reacted to the processes of socialist development in Cuba despite concerted efforts by the U.S. government to thwart research and scholarship (Fuller 1988). Cuban studies have evolved from fairly limited investigations of elite-mass relationships to more detailed examinations of the institutional processes of policymaking and implementation (Valdéz 1988; Benglesdorf 1988a). These latter approaches include pathbreaking works on socialist legality by Salas (1979b) and Azicri (1980a; 1980c), labor policy by Pérez-Stable (1986), professional development by Fitzgerald (1990b), health-care policy by Santana (1987) and Feinsilver (1989a), housing by Hamberg (1986), and community mental health by García-Averasturi (1985) and Camayd-Freixas and Uriarte (1980). These studies encompass broader processes in which citizens become recipients or consumers of health care and other social services; fulfill social, occupational, and political roles (which sometimes come into conflict); and behave as a subject of rights and duties governed by social norms and legal institutions.

In this regard, a primary objective of Cuban socialism has been to reconstitute its citizens by providing common learning experiences that enable them to achieve a high degree of revolutionary integration. This entails removing discordant, inconsistent, prerevolutionary beliefs and attitudes that undermine the pursuit of new national goals and strengthening citizen's capacity to deal with stress and uncertainty. We can gauge Cuba's progress toward attaining socialist development goals through the study of strategies that attempt to redefine the cultural context and aims of individual behavior.

Informal Networks and Political Factions

When society undergoes transition during periods of political upheaval and cultural change, the relationships among legal status, social class, and occupational role change, sometimes altering systems of respect and contempt and fundamentally redistributing the burdens and benefits among its citizens (Galanter 1966; Wiarda 1971). In Cuba, for example, property and other assets were confiscated from businesses, middle-class professionals could no longer find work in their fields, and certain forms of private conduct were criminalized (Azicri 1981). According to Sampson (1985:46), socialist states undergoing transitions such as these are particularly vulnerable to the growth of informal networks because they provide an alternative method of allocating resources and thus "compete with traditional bureaucratic means of redistribution" monopolized by the state.

Studies by Yang (1989) and Lewis (1986) in China and Shlapentokh (1989) and Willerton (1992) in the Soviet Union indicate that network analysis can provide insights about the processes of policymaking in one-party-dominated socialist states. Social networks consist of interactions (involving communication and the exchange of information, resources, influence, and other social goods) between persons who perform institutional roles that vary in terms of proximity and access to centers of decisionmaking for the allocation and distribution of scarce resources. Network analysis seeks to identify how the form (i.e., frequency of contact, degree of joint involvement, and density or number of intermediate connections) of interactions affects the outcomes of governance and policymaking processes (Burt and Minor 1983; Knoke 1990; Marsden and Lin 1982).

Informal exchange structures are not necessarily regime threatening, according to Sampson, as they can be enlisted "benignly" by the state to bypass sometimes ponderous and inefficient official channels. Nevertheless, corruption can reach epidemic proportions, as Millar (1988) illustrates, when Leonid Brezhnev cut a "little deal" with *nalevos*, private networks of distribution not subject to party or state regulation, in order to ease shortages by allowing them to compete with party-dominated government suppliers of consumer items. Millar contends that this policy contributed to the political crisis in the Soviet Union and undermined Mikhail Gorbachev's attempt to implement economic reforms because his strategy failed to resolve the underlying disparities in political power and influence sustained by communist rule.

Cuban social analyst Dr. Fernando Barral argues, according to Grogg (1991), that the alarming growth of a "second economy" in Cuba, based on the emergence of a "mercantilist mentality," first witnessed in the Soviet Union under *perestroika*, is now threatening the integrity of "social distribution as a whole" in Cuba. This book examines the economic conditions and psychological factors that have contributed to the growth and transformation of informal networks in Cuba and gauges their effect on the processes of social reconstruction.

The collapse of Communist Party rule in Eastern European countries such as Czechoslovakia, Poland, and the Baltic states has been attributed to the absence of a civil society, or a domain of private conduct or collective action relatively free from control by the party or state apparatus. Nevertheless, strategic opposition by such groups as Solidarity in Poland, Charter 77 in Czechoslovakia, and the National Independence Movement in Lithuania (Oleszczuk 1988) was effective, in part, because of the coordination and unification of extensive informal networks of workers and dissidents into a collective instrument for mass political action.

Networks can take on system-threatening proportions when linkages are forged between or among disparate political or rights groups by what Oleszczuk (1988:55) calls "hybrid dissidents." These political activists, whose interests cut across different issues, helped unite groups with disparate causes in Lithuania, thereby thwarting official tactics of selective repression. Once Gorbachev acknowledged the right of Baltic states to negotiate independence in 1987, Lithuanian rights groups mounted a successful independence movement that culminated in Soviet withdrawal and national autonomy. By comparison, dissident rights groups in Cuba are small and fragmented. Nevertheless, there are signs that such groups are attempting to join forces in an attempt to strengthen their influence with the Cuban leadership.

Representing Social Interests: Mass Organizations and Professionals

Socialist regimes such as Cuba's have never officially recognized or permitted the organization of independent interest groups. Instead, party-sponsored mass organizations were created to promote citizen participation and were invested with authority to implement specific policies. Although differing in certain essential respects from their American counterparts, Cuban mass organizations such as the FMC have evolved to play roles that resemble some aspects of state regulatory agencies in the United States. They are mandated by the Cuban Constitution to represent specific interests, such as those involved in the protection of the health and welfare of children or public safety. Mass organizations rely on education and regulation to accomplish these mandates. The CDRs excelled early in administering public health campaigns (e.g., inoculations, sanitation) and crime-control activities. This contributed to a dramatic increase in their political influence in provincial and national policymaking and administrative bodies (Domínguez 1978:260–67). Moreover, the CDRs flourished during the early period of mobilization because they enlisted, by far, the most participants, a primary criterion of success in the early years of the revolution.

A number of structural features of Cuban mass organizations distinguish them from U.S. interest groups: State sponsorship entails obvious constraints on the span of issue control, expression of opposition to policy, and range of action. Membership is induced, although participation is voluntary. Top leadership is selected by party officials, whereas lower-level positions are awarded on the basis of the extent of service. Mass organizations are recognized as constitutional entities, although their specific positions and influence within the governmental bureaucracy are subject to change over time. In this regard, the head of the Women's Federation, Vilma Espín (1991), Raúl Castro's wife, served as a member of the Politburo, the highest decisionmaking body in Cuba, until pressure was mounted for her resignation in 1991. In comparison, the CDRs have experienced a general decline in political influence, a trend that began in 1970 and was accentuated in 1976 by the development of mechanisms of local governance.

In other respects, mass organizations do possess some degree of independent initiative and leverage over policies, and they engage in strategic action involving the generation of information and support for policy. Mass organizations have been able to develop an identity and a record of accomplishments over time, which speak against their being contrivances of the party. The criteria by which the activities of mass organizations have been judged appear to have changed over time. Information, expertise, and capability for long-term problem solving have assumed greater importance in the fortunes of the mass organization. Congresses are now convened in which more time is devoted to discussion of studies conducted by experts than to consideration of alternative strategies. With this emergent situation, successful leadership of mass organizations now depends on the formation of mutually beneficial relationships with party officials, government agencies, and, especially, professionals involved in the delivery of services.

In this regard, there are at least four factors that influence the role of lawyers, doctors, psychologists, and other mental health professionals in socialist regimes undergoing the processes of economic and political development. They are the following: (1) adaptability to new ideological orientations and roles, (2) the extent of institutional control and organizational strength of the profession, (3) the flexibility of its methods of practice and effectiveness in problem solving, and (4) the degree of support from leaders of the intelligentsia and other segments of society (Solomon 1978:156–59; Kozulin 1984:5–34; Freidson 1986; and Krause 1991:4–11). Unlike their Western counterparts, professionals in socialist states do not possess organizational independence. Consequently, the identity and degree of authority professionals acquire depend upon their capacity to deal successfully in bureaucratic politics dominated by party officials.

Intellectuals, artists, and dissidents have come to play decisive roles in promoting political and social reforms in authoritarian socialist regimes in Eastern Europe through oppositional strategies designed to under-mine official policies (Stromas 1979:222). In contrast, professionals in law, medicine, education, and engineering have played a more ambiguous, less decisive role in the rejection of Communist Party rule and in the sup-port of democratic forces (Jones and Krause 1991). For example, physi-cians and health-care workers in Poland were unable alone to secure in-dependence from communist domination without help from Solidarity, which sought concessions in the form of improvements in medical care (Kennedy and Sadkowski 1991).

Regime authority and control may become destabilized when the center of gravity of policymaking processes changes, as in Cuba, where the Communist Party assumed policy leadership as well as control of all administrative functions. This substantially altered mechanisms of authority, partisan representation, and legal and constitutional relation-ships. Under such conditions, new modes of access and influence must be mastered by any who seek representation in the new order. The un-wieldy system of centralized planning adopted in the early 1960s gave way to a decentralized system in 1976 largely because party cadres did not possess sufficient expertise to manage resources and services effectively. Consequently, in the 1976 Cuban constitution the Cuban Communist Party (PCC) was divested of its operational, administrative role, and a new system of governance was created that increased local participation and accountability. The Cuban regime has undergone a number of such destabilizing episodes since the onset of the revolution. These episodes constitute critical junctures in which strategic relation-ships undergo alterations that redistribute the balance of forces advanc-ing and impeding the processes of social reconstruction.

Discursive Knowledge and Social Discipline

One difficulty faced by modern regimes whose economic systems are based upon universalistic (i.e., equality of social needs and human dignity), rather than particularistic (i.e., reward according to class posi-tion or patronage), criteria of distribution is that they must rely, in part, on objective and impartial judgments by professionals or bureaucrats to formulate policies for the common good. This is so because individuals differ extensively in terms of the kind of assistance and services they re-quire to attain some common standard of well-being (Elster and Roemer 1991). Critics point out, however, that decisions about the distribution of services grounded in either professional or bureaucratic judgment consti-tute a disguised paternalism (Foucault 1980; Kleinig 1983), obscuring the boundaries between authority and power, rights and social norms (i.e., expectations about appropriate conduct), and modes of governance and discipline that help distinguish between authoritarian and democratic societies governed by consent and the rule of law.

Foucault (1980:106–8), an unflinching critic of modernity, contends that discourse about social needs has so penetrated the realm of behavior heretofore considered free from interference that disciplinary techniques of control and normalization have now problematically displaced juridical systems of sovereignty and rights. Regimes that derive normative judgments about social conduct from universalistic criteria of well-being tend to rely on strategies of prevention to regulate and control conduct. This occurs because the maintenance of societal well-being encompasses a broad range of behavioral capacities and tendencies considered either potentially valuable or deleterious to society. Thus, efforts to promote well-being by curbing behavior deemed unhealthy considerably narrow the scope of legally permissible activity. Foucault has demonstrated how the attributes and effects of power extend well beyond the domain legitimated by modern political systems predicated on the concept of limited government, consent, and the primacy of individual rights. He urges us to conceive of power, not as some limited resource concentrated among the few to dominate, control, and exploit others, but as a dynamic force that is dispersed and circulated through institutional structures composed of asymmetrical and unstable strategic relationships.

Foucault conceives of power in terms of an ever-shifting field of strategic relationships (a conception compatible with network analysis) in which the recipients of disciplinary control seek to modify or evade techniques designed to confine or regulate their actions and to override or replace the systems of reward and retribution by which their behavior is normalized and judged. A strategic relationship, as Foucault defines it, involves indirect tactics in which adversaries attempt to control or influence the field of action and probable sequence of ensuing events. Power is not a mechanism of control, according to Foucault (1982:221), but embodies specific forms that strategic interaction assumes "within a more or less open field of possibilities." Power, therefore, does not consist of unilateral confrontation and success, defeat, or withdrawal; rather, it consists of an everchanging pattern of actions, reactions, and counterreactions. Foucault (1982:222) expresses the *agonistic* relationship between power and freedom by saying, "At the very heart of the power relationship, and constantly provoking it, are the recalcitrance of the will and the intransigence of freedom. Rather than speaking of an essential freedom it would be better to speak of an "agonism"—of a relationship that is the same time reciprocal incitation and struggle; less of a face to face confrontation that paralyzes both sides than a permanent provocation."

One of the ideas that Castro finds most objectionable about the Western discourse on rights and consent is the declaration that regime support be conditional. However, support can never be conditional in a regime based on sacrifice for the common good. Castro's statement that everything is possible *within* the revolution draws attention to the fact that regime legitimacy is not at stake when someone evades compliance, commits crimes, or criticizes the leadership. While these acts of defiance or resistance challenge authority, they do nothing to stop the ongoing processes of reconstruction. Instead, the legitimacy of the Cuban revolution is truly threatened when citizens refuse to struggle and endure the agony of being involved in a strategic situation whose parameters are unclear and whose outcome is uncertain. Foucault's characterization of power as embodying an agonistic relationship seems pertinent to the Cuban experience because Castro has continuously attempted to strategically redefine the parameters of struggle (i.e., by reorganizing the field of possible action and redefining the roles played by the participants) so that the center of gravity in policy implementation is always shifting and changing from one site and group of decisionmakers to another. Consequently, all those engaged in the processes of social reconstruction must continually anticipate and adapt to the opportunities and potential difficulties each new policy poses before getting a handle on how it affects the existing roles and patterns of power.

Foucault describes how three new social forces emerged in the eighteenth and nineteenth centuries to completely revolutionize the conventional, juridical conception of governance. First, the classical conception of sovereignty, which was based on the monarch's absolute power over his subjects, was replaced by representative systems based on the protection of individual rights and government by consent. These grew out of new economic practices based on markets and property ownership that were introduced in the eighteenth century. However, the principles of efficiency and utilitarianism (i.e., the greatest good for the greatest number) quickly penetrated political discourse and juridical practices to bring about a transformation of state responsibilities for the promotion of social welfare and rehabilitation of criminal offenders. Foucault (1979:104–30) contends that during this nineteenth-century reform era, which was led by Jeremy Bentham and John Stuart Mill, schools, hospitals, prisons, and other social institutions were redesigned for the more efficient management and control of the recipients of public services. Consequently, Foucault continues, techniques were introduced to "individualize" persons by examining, sorting, and classifying them according to age, competence, health, offense, and other biological or environmental differences so that they could be more effectively trained to behave and work according to the norms of performance established by all others similarly situated and classified.

Second, advances in the biological sciences generated knowledge and medical techniques that made possible dramatic improvements in individual well-being, longevity, and public health (Foucault 1973). This development not only aided in the bureaucratic classification and differentiation of individuals according to specific traits, tendencies, susceptibilities, capacities, and so forth, but also greatly facilitated the detection, control, treatment, and prevention of disease and mental disorders.

Third, kinship systems based on paternalism and sexual prohibitions were undermined by psychoanalytic theory, which discovered that sexuality was a form of energy (i.e., libido) that could be harnessed and deployed to alter the relationships of power among parents, children, and the state (Foucault 1978:135–43). The confluence of these changes resulted in what Foucault characterizes as the invasion or colonization of the realm of law and rights by a social discourse based on scientific norms and clinical techniques of intervention and control (Foucault 1980:107).

In their drive for development, socialist states, such as China during Mao's leadership, have attempted to extend the reach of the state into almost every recess of society and consciousness. Nevertheless, civil society still occupies an irrepressible space no matter how tightly the official mechanisms of social control are drawn. Yang (1989) persuasively demonstrates the insights that a Foucaultian perspective can yield in understanding the complex relationships of power and resistance between the official and informal sectors involved in the implementation of Chinese social policies. Yang illustrates how the practice of *guanxi*, or gift economy, subverts the effectiveness of disciplinary and normalizing techniques employed in China to regulate and control the population. As an illicit form of exchange, *guanxi* reverses the power differential conferred by party membership, official authority, or other criteria by implicating recipients of higher status in a complex scheme in which repayment is contingent on acts that confer, deny, or restore "face" (i.e., a sense of respect, security, and well-being) for the donor. This exchange of symbolic political capital undermines the norms of conduct by which status is bestowed in state redistributive economies.

Although Foucault's thesis about the sequence through which the modern state emerged remains controversial, Cuba has had to confront many of the same challenges and dilemmas of authority and discipline, justice and community, that face developed and developing nations involved in the transition from traditionalism to modernity (Connolly 1987). Castro insists that the Cuban revolution has always been guided by the principles of Marxism-Leninism, which hold that social injustice and imperialism are the consequences of a capitalist system dominanted by a ruling class. Even though these principles have provided general guidelines for the redistribution of wealth and reorganization of the

Cuban economy (i.e., state ownership and planning), the processes of social reconstruction in Cuba do not appear to have followed the sequence of change predicted by Karl Marx, nor has Cuba's changing status in the world economy conformed precisely to the imperatives of imperialism predicted by V.I. Lenin. For example, work is rewarded, not according to need, but according to ability or contribution; and Cuba's precarious situation in the current world economic order stems partly from the collapse of communism rather than solely from the persistence of the U.S. economic blockade.

The Cuban leadership seeks to dispense with classical and liberal conceptions of sovereignty, rights, and consent in order to reconstruct economic, legal, and social institutions according to conceptions of sacrifice, civic virtue, and well-being. For example, Cuba's experiment in popular justice, discussed in Chapter 2, embodied the attempt to transform punishment for economic crimes against the state into a pedagogical instrument to redefine the norms by which an individual would be judged under socialism. In addition, new techniques of work discipline continue to be explored (see Chapter 3) to sustain increased productivity by using moral, nonmaterial incentives and rewards based on one's conduct within the group and contribution to society as a whole.

But Cuban policymakers discovered in the second decade of the revolution that the struggle for social justice must devolve to the family, where child development, attitude formation, and role acquisition become crucial determinants of the possibility of further social reconstruction. As chapters 4 and 6 illustrate, the psychological study of individuals working cooperatively in groups while under stress is generating norms and techniques to harness and channel the capacity for self-criticism and sacrifice into more flexible and productive modes of discipline. Finally, in Chapter 7, we glimpse how successive changes in health care have attempted to get medicine to implement a broader conception of its preventive mission and find promising but risky applications of biotechnology to strengthen Cubans in their continued struggle to overcome the psychological and physiological forces that block transformation.

The capacity to learn through struggle has contributed to an ability of the Cuban leadership and people to recover from the many mistakes and reversals illustrated in the policies examined in this book. The willingness to succeed against all odds is perhaps best captured by the phrase uttered by many Cubans: "It can be resolved." Cuba's resiliency demonstrates the effectiveness of the application of the logic of struggle to problem solving: The resolution of one set of problems results in a new set of contingencies and uncertainties, and learning embodied in a strategic relationship consists of being prepared to anticipate the unexpected rather than the familiar and routine.

This book focuses on the strengths and vulnerabilities (or dilemmas) of three interrelated dimensions of the Cuban revolutionary struggle for independence. First, a psychological struggle is being waged by Cubans to adopt unselfish attitudes and behave according to group norms of conduct without slipping into modes of discipline that constrain behavior and diminish the capacity of the individual to exercise independent judgment. Second, a political struggle is being waged to develop a system of governance based, not upon sovereignty and rights, but upon a conception of well-being. The difficulty involved in using societal health as the basis of regime legitimation is a tendency toward paternalism and a risk of condemnation by the international community for failure to respect the principles of limited government and the inviolability of individual rights. Finally, there is an ongoing historical and cultural struggle to overcome the cycle of reform and retrenchment in which optimism about the future is replaced by cynicism and a return to the past. Success in overcoming this cycle requires the effective resolution of microsocial struggles that include machismo, stereotyped gender and family roles, workplace discrimination, bureaucratization, and related problems that block the transition from patrimonialism and particularism to a universalistic regime based on the humane application of scientific advances, respect for life, and human dignity.

Part 1

The Struggle for Justice
and Discipline

1

Conciencia, Lucha, *and*
Social Transformation

The strategies for social transformation pursued in Cuba strongly reflect the experiences and personalities of Fidel Castro and Che Guevara. Castro's own psychological and moral development was a product of the conflict and resistance he faced in attempting to live up to the ideals embodied in his Jesuit upbringing. Castro conceived of *conciencia* as a provocation to resist selfishness and a willingness to endure the agonistic processes involved in overcoming the economic and social contradictions of dependency and self-doubt that block the path to socialist development. This scenario for self-transformation required a rejection of material reward, a highly developed sense of justice, and a willingness to sacrifice oneself for an ideal.

As a physician, Guevara developed a fascination with people struggling to cope with and overcome immune disorders such as leprosy and cancer. Guevara believed that the creation of socialist persons entailed a similar struggle to cope with uncertainty and stress. *Lucha* was not used by Guevara exclusively as a synonym for warfare; he also used the word to describe how the experience of hardship and self-denial could contribute to the psychobiological transformation of the human being. Guevara believed that physicians trained in social medicine would continue the revolution initiated by the guerrillas to hasten the transformation of people under socialism.

The *guerrilla foco* provided the strategic context in which *conciencia* and *lucha* would coalesce to produce new people capable of great courage and sacrifice. As Debray (1967:102–3, 106) observes, the *foco* was conceived as a holistic, biological concept. It constituted the nucleus of a new social and economic order. The *foco* also yielded a number of principles and techniques with which to continue the process of revolutionary social reconstruction following the insurrection.

Finally, the Cuban revolution sought not only to end a dictatorship but also to overcome the forces of colonialism and imperialism that compromised Cuba's independence as a sovereign state. U.S. hostility and the maintenance of an economic blockade for more than thirty years necessitated long-term trade agreements with and loans from the Soviet Union and Eastern Europe. The defense of the Cuban revolution has also included an internationalist strategy that has evolved from support of revolutionary movements in the Third World to civilian technical assistance and the peaceful transfer of technology and capital to the developing world. The strategies governing Cuban internationalism have been adapted to reflect changes in geopolitics and the world economy as well as to complement and reinforce changing economic priorities and policies for national development.

The Jesuit Origins of Conciencia

Castro recounted the formative influence of Catholicism on his early development in unusually candid terms in a lengthy interview with Frei Betto in 1986. Castro's recollections of his youth provide a window through which we can glimpse the psychological and experiential roots of his conception of *conciencia*. Castro admitted to having rebelled at an early age in a rigidly disciplinarian home, which resulted in his placement in a boarding school run by Dominicans (Betto 1987:113). Ironically, he welcomed this as a step toward "freedom," even though it was a challenging and frustrating stage in his development.

His experience at the La Salle School proved to be a disheartening one. In fifth grade, Castro learned how wealth and class contributed to favoritism among the students. He also was the frequent subject of corporal punishment, which Castro felt to be an "inconceivable" affront to his sense of personal dignity. Castro explained in retrospect that he reacted negatively to a system that required an unequivocal and unquestioning compliance because "it is impossible to develop the reasoning and feelings that could be the basis of sincere religious belief" (Betto 1987:118). To act out of fear or the desire for reward did not constitute a legitimate basis of personal esteem or admiration. Respect was reserved only for those who followed their convictions, according to Castro, despite the risk and personal cost (Betto 1987:124–25).

The following year, Castro started attending a Jesuit school that led to his acceptance at the Colegio de Belén in Havana. Castro was impressed by the priests' strong character, austerity, and self-discipline, and he admired their compassion, fairness, and sense of justice. The Jesuit techniques of character development were predicated upon an entirely different notion of conscience than had been the case at previous schools. Acts of conscience need not be triggered by reactive feelings of shame, guilt, or false pride but could involve great feats of courage and heroism, motivated by feelings of compassion and a strong intolerance of injustice (Betto 1987:140–42). This conception of conscience offered Castro a way to channel his recalcitrance and rebelliousness constructively. Castro candidly admitted that his own and humankind's natural rebelliousness made Marxism a particularly appealing theory of revolution. Marxism not only revealed the causes of injustice in the exploitation of labor but also provided a theory to guide conscience (Betto 1987:145). Consequently, a successful strategy for "carrying out a deep social revolution," according to Castro, must help the Cuban people focus their discontent by enabling them to correctly perceive world imperialism as the source of injustice.

During his Jesuit education, Castro was exposed to the philosophical ideas of great Catholic thinkers such as St. Augustine and St. Thomas Aquinas (Donahue 1963). These and other medieval philosophers were preoccupied with defining the relationship between *synderesis* (reason) and *conciencia* (conscience). Aquinas, in particular, attempted to overcome a paradox that had perplexed his predecessors: How is it possible to act and be bound by conscience and yet sometimes violate conventional reason and truth? Aquinas resolved this issue by arguing that conscience, unlike reason, could be actualized only through acts of will requiring a conscious choice with real consequences.

As MacIntyre (1988:189) observes, Aquinas's account stresses that judgment is contingent and circumstantial and that our moral character is defined as much by our practical actions as by our precepts. This led Aquinas to argue that a sense of justice cannot be acquired solely by reasoning about the conditions of fairness or equality but must involve an existential act to overcome physical and emotional barriers that inhibit our capacity to treat all humans with dignity. Castro would have found this ethic appealing because it encouraged an experimental attitude. It suggested that human nature could be reshaped under socialism by a concerted application of new scientific methods to change the psychological and social circumstances of existence. Castro was convinced that the "underdevelopment in revolutionary ideas" stemmed from faulty methods of inquiry. He urged that

> we must analyze contemporary phenomena, study them profoundly. Naturally such analyses, such concepts must be more and the more the work of groups rather than individuals. Just as in scientific fields the isolated researcher scarcely any longer exists, nor can he so exist in politics, in economics, in sociology, isolated researchers—the appearance of people of genius under modern conditions—becomes more and more improbable. (1968:193)

Guevara and the Logic of Struggle

It is doubtful whether Castro could or would have fully embraced and implemented moral incentives during the initial years of social reconstruction without Guevara's supreme confidence in the feasibility of such measures. Guevara helped Castro overcome his own doubts as well as extensive opposition among old-line communists such as Anabal Escalante. Importantly, Guevara articulated a process by which the person, "the unfinished product" of an exploitative world, could be transformed through the development of consciousness into "a new socialist being." In his famous essay, "Notes on Man in Socialism," Guevara (1968e:390–91) denied the necessity of a period of transition in which an economic crisis would render capitalism obsolete. Instead, Guevara believed it was possible to skip this stage by creating a new person and new forms of production simultaneously. To accomplish this, society as a whole would have to become "a huge school," Guevara (1968e:393) reasoned, so that the development of new values and attitudes would coincide with a structure of production liberated from necessity.

Guevara's conception of development captured the essence of *lucha*, or the logic of struggle. It signified, not an escape into a self-indulgent freedom, but the embrace of an existence in which "its cadres must be full professors of assiduity and sacrifice" (Guevara 1968e:397). The new person formed one of two "pillars" of socialist society; technology formed the other. New technologies could be fashioned that would reintegrate the person with his or her environment, enabling the experience of reenchantment with work as a creative enterprise. Guevara (1968a:114–15) believed that social medicine would furnish techniques to achieve this goal. The practice of scientific social medicine, if founded on principles of social ecology, epidemiology, and prevention, could bring about the psychobiological and moral transformation of the Cuban people. Guevara (1968e:397) best expressed this goal in his metaphor of "society giving birth to a new being" who would be "free from original sin" by being shorn of cultural trappings acquired during years of domination under imperialism.

As a physician, Guevara was particularly sensitive to gross inequities in the distribution of medical care in Latin America and seeming indifference to research and actions that might eradicate malnutrition and tropical diseases that victimized thousands of impoverished infants and children. These strong feelings made it impossible for him to pursue his aspiration of "becoming a famous scientist or making a significant contribution to medical science" (Guevara 1968a:112). Guevara's lifelong battle with asthma led to a fascination with the psychosomatic dimensions of allergies (a subject of his medical thesis) and possible methods to overcome this disability (Ebon 1967:24, 133–40). Guevara spent a considerable amount of time studying victims of leprosy in Peru, Brazil, and Venezuela and providing psychotherapy for them (Ebon 1967:19, 21; Koningsberger 1971:19–20). Apparently, he had a strong interest in understanding factors that weaken or contribute to the breakdown of the human immune system, making the individual susceptible to diseases such as leprosy and cancer. According to one of his closest friends, biochemist Dr. Alberto Granados, when Guevara's mother contracted cancer, he undertook an extended series of experiments with guinea pigs, hoping desperately that he might discover a cure (Ebon 1967:14). These formative experiences and interests help explain Guevara's insistence that a new person would have to be created with intestinal fortitude strong enough to immunize him or her against the deforming forces of imperialism and inescapable stress involved in the long struggle for independence, dignity, and self-respect.

The logic of struggle provided an exemplar or prototype of the processes through which all Cubans could shed the physical habits and psychological dependency associated with underdevelopment. The acquisition of revolutionary consciousness required the participant to wage war against self-doubt and seek salvation in sacrifice. Guevara (1985:52, 78–79) argued that the heroic guerrilla exhibited an "asceticism" and a "stoicism that show him to be a true priest of reform" and a "Jesuit of warfare."

Guevara's mixing of religious and military metaphors draws attention to a facet of the ethic of sacrifice that invests it with such enormous power; that is, its effectiveness as an instrument to induce collective behavior. Foucault (1982:214) observes that the early Christians may have been the first to gain insights as to how salvation could be used as an effective instrument of governance in the premodern state. Foucault contends that the Christian ethic of sacrifice helped bring about a regime of "pastoral power" based, not on sovereignty and right, but on truth and salvation. Pastoral power is derived from a holistic conception of society, the cohesion of which depends on consistent devotion to the needs of each of its members. Sacrifice is not demanded for defense of a sovereign but for the persistence of a way of life whose existence can be extinguished only if there is a general failure of the will to resist the temptations of self-indulgence and greed.

Pastoralism is a form of power that cannot be exercised, as Foucault points out, "without knowing the inside of people's minds," their "souls," and "their innermost secrets." The essence of pastoral power is that "it implies a knowledge of the conscience and the ability to direct it" (Foucault 1982:214). Foucault believes that pastoral power is the precursor to modern (i.e., disciplinary) forms of power because it is predicated on norms of conduct and techniques of self-control (i.e., confession and repentance) whereby individuals must live up to and abide by the truths of conscience in exchange for redemption. However, according to Foucault (1982:214–15), because salvation has been replaced by the secular aim of perpetuating life and promoting individual well-being in the modern state, disciplinary control consists of getting individuals to adopt behavior considered appropriate to the truths science reveals about their biological and psychological development.

The Guerrilla Foco

One of the critical challenges Castro and his guerrilla movement faced in launching a successful insurrection in Cuba was to develop a strategy capable not only of defeating Batista's army but also of generating popular support for a revolutionary transformation of Cuban politics and society. The absence of well-organized and disciplined party cadres forced Castro to adopt strategies different from those of an urban-based revolution. The strategy of *foco*, or using the guerrilla as the focus of political and military operations, was adopted to find avenues through which the poverty and underdevelopment characteristic of rural Cuba could find political expression. The success of the *guerrilla foco* did not rest exclusively on military tactics but involved a campaign to consolidate political opposition against Fulgencio Batista's dictatorship.

Castro believed that a successful revolutionary war could not be waged by guerrillas in cities and urban areas because they would be limited to random acts of terrorism. The tactics by which the principles of a new social order were to be introduced had to be implemented and tested within an isolated environment susceptible to fairly complete control. For example, during the initial stages of the insurrection, when guerrilla forces were small and security was the utmost priority, tactics involving secrecy, deceit, fear, and reprisal were crucial to their survival. Significantly, Castro capitalized on peasant resentment of landowners and distrust of the regular military by designating casualties of Batista's troops as martyrs while branding peasants executed by the guerrillas as traitors (Bonachea and San Martin 1974:91). This peremptory and summary mode of operation was eventually replaced by a code and system of revolutionary justice that served as a precursor to the experiment in popular justice (Van der Plas 1987).

One organizational tactic of overriding strategic importance to the success of the insurrection was the creation of secure areas, or "zones of defense." These locales served as supply bases and staging areas for military maneuvers. In principle, each zone had to be self-sustaining but trade and exchange were permitted between them (Guevara 1985:

120–27). The defense zones were able to coordinate and conceal their military operations largely by replacing entrepreneurial middle-men with guerrillas who assumed the role of intermediary among peasants, landowners, and anyone else beyond. This tactic enabled the guerrillas to extend their span of social control and political influence through a communication network far beyond their military capabilities (Bonachea and San Martin 1974:181–84).

Castro's luck and genius enabled him to forge a network of political support from other competing resistance groups without forfeiting control over the political objectives of the insurrection. Castro selected skillful intermediaries such as Celia Sánchez and Vilma Espín to generate knowledge about the motives, interests, and agendas of competing political factions indispensable to the consolidation of political support necessary to maintain leadership of the Cuban revolution. Castro's success in achieving his conception of a just social order during subsequent phases of the revolution has turned upon his continued ability to make the most effective use of party cadres, professionals, and other intermediaries engaged in the tasks of generating support for his policies.

Internationalism and Struggle

The Cuban insurrection marked only the initial stage of a long, open-ended struggle for national independence. The short-term survival of the first socialist state in the Western Hemisphere depended profoundly on its ability to obtain immediate political support and financial aid from the Soviet Union and favored trade status with Eastern Europe. The enormity of Soviet subsidies and technical assistance in the first two and one-half decades of the revolution (the precipitous withdrawal of which has triggered an economic crisis in Cuba) popularized the thesis that Cuban internationalism was a surrogate for Soviet foreign policy during the cold war. Consequently, critics were unwilling to acknowledge the authenticity and distinctiveness of Cuba's strategy against imperialism and dependency (Valdéz 1988:195).

The Cuban struggle for national independence is historically intertwined with the battle to overcome U.S. domination and economic exploitation. The nineteenth-century Cuban revolutionary José Martí correctly perceived the political subjugation lurking in economic dependency and foresaw the moral dimensions of the conflict that would have to be waged to achieve national unity before attaining national independence (Kirk 1983; Pérez-Stable 1990). Martí's conception of *sociabilidad* (social solidarity) succinctly captured the dual moral imperatives of shared adversity and mutual assistance that each Cuban must observe in his or her quest to repudiate the divisiveness and distrust engendered by

U.S. intervention (Kirk 1983:92–93). Castro attempted to demonstrate that these principles can serve as the basis of international solidarity among Third World countries seeking independence without risking economic collapse.

As noted before, the notion of a *guerrilla foco* made an original and innovative revision to orthodox Marxist-Leninist theories regarding the necessary sequence of socialist development. The catalyst for civil revolt need not involve a highly organized and united political party or a protracted economic crisis. The adoption of an ethic of sacrifice and the implementation of the logic of struggle were sufficient to set the forces of social reconstruction in motion. Nevertheless, the ideal communist society was unlikely to be realized in developing countries like Cuba unless they ended economic dependency on Western capitalist states. The Soviet Union was able to resolve this problem temporarily by endorsing, in Joseph Stalin's words, "socialism in one country" and by sealing off its post—World War II satellites in a self-contained but woefully inefficient and uncompetitive economic partnership.

Castro (1968:40–45) condemned as shortsighted the belief that socialism could coexist with imperialism. He denied that there was any one correct socialist formula; that could be determined only through experiment and experience. Moreover, he challenged the belief that communism could be constructed in one country as long as the immense and inequitable asymmetry in the distribution of capital and technology persisted between the developed and underdeveloped world. While it might be possible to conduct socialist experiments, Castro (1968:45) insisted that "communism as a formula of absolute abundance, in the midst of an underdeveloped world, cannot be built in a single country without running the risk, involuntarily and unintentionally, in future years of immensely rich countries finding themselves trading and dealing with immensely poor countries."

The rationale for Cuban internationalism, as Castro conceived it, was to ensure that socialism brought about the simultaneous development of all underdeveloped countries. Socialist states could not afford to forfeit the moral superiority that their ideology of equality and dignity of persons represented and still retain leadership of world revolutionary movements. By this reckoning, Cuban leadership in the Third World provided a kind of moral leverage over the Soviet Union (and Western capitalist states) to increase its aid to Cuba in order to retain influence over the direction of incipient movements for national independence emerging around the world. But Cuba's long-term survival could not be guaranteed by Soviet subsidy alone: Development required diversification, technological innovation, and mutually beneficial terms of trade. As Erisman

(1985) observes, Cuba had to mount a strategy of "counterdependency" in order to continuously enlarge the space in which to maneuver.

Cuba's foreign policy in the 1960s reflected Castro's and Guevara's ambitions to lead the Third World in an armed struggle against imperialism. Castro (1968:117–21) made an impassioned plea at the first meeting of the Organization of Latin American States to learn from the Cuban experience and courageously undertake struggles for national independence. Similarly, in 1967 Guevara (1985:209) urged participants of the Tricontinental Conference of the Organization of Solidarity of Peoples of Africa, Asia, and Latin America to force the United States to fight multiple Vietnamese-type guerrilla engagements to bring about the collapse of U.S. hegemony in world politics. Guevara inspired Cuban-supported insurgencies in several Central and South American countries, including Guatemala, El Salvador, Venezuela, Colombia, and Peru, and he personally directed the guerrilla conflict in Bolivia that resulted in his untimely death in 1967.

These forays into international politics seriously alienated Latin American leaders while straining Cuba's relationship with the Soviet Union. Consequently, after 1968 Cuba gradually assumed a less militant posture. Cuba no longer instigated conflict but instead supported indigenous national liberation movements, such as those in Nicaragua, Grenada, and Angola, that shared the objectives of socialist internationalism. This brought about a rapprochement with the Soviet leadership, resulting in greater consonance and collaboration in foreign policy (Domínguez 1989b:142–46).

Cuba's international strategy has undergone significant change since the early 1970s. Greater emphasis has been placed on civilian assistance than on militarism. Cuban internationalism is now guided by pragmatic considerations involving the creation of reciprocal but flexible relations with other countries (Domínguez 1989b). Cuba exports its expertise and resources for social development to other countries with which it shares ideological objectives, diplomatic relations, or trade agreements. Cuba also continues to carry an enormous multi-billion-dollar debt to the Soviet Union and other trading partners. This exerts a tremendous drag on the Cuban economy, which can be offset in part by the contribution of labor in exchange for foreign currency. For example, between fourteen thousand and twenty thousand construction workers served in building brigades abroad from 1974 to 1980 (Eckstein 1988:157). Cuba tried to offset balance-of-trade deficits by sending workers to Eastern European countries such as Czechoslovakia and to other members of the Council for Mutual Economic Assistance, but these arrangements have been discontinued since the collapse of the communist leadership in Eastern Europe.

To be sure, Cuba is seeking new trading partners in Latin America and elsewhere to avert potential economic collapse, but this will not be an easy task given the tightening of the U.S. blockade and a shortage of hard currency (Zimbalist 1992).

In 1979, Castro inaugurated a new strategy for Third World development predicated on the principle of "world economic interdependency." In a speech to the thirty-seventh session of the United Nations General Assembly, Castro (1981:202–7) outlined a comprehensive plan by which technology and financial assistance could be provided to promote economic development. He recommended that a fund of approximately $350 billion be created and administered by the United Nations Industrial and Economic Development Organization (Castro 1981:205–6). A significant portion of these funds would be earmarked to support the kinds of social and medical services that Cuba is now providing to more than thirty countries in Africa, Asia, and the Middle East (Díaz Briquets and Pérez-López 1989). Thus, Cuba stands to benefit substantially by such schemes by virtue of having its personnel already in place to become recipients of development aid. Castro underscored the urgency for increased economic assistance in 1983 by declaring that the enormous financial debt incurred by Latin American and other Third World countries was unrepayable and should be canceled. Instead, Castro (1983a:23–27, 215–16) presciently called for a "new international economic order" led by the United Nations to rectify the persistent problems of underdevelopment faced by the majority of countries in the world.

Castro has skillfully orchestrated an ongoing strategy to deflect the campaign mounted by the United States under the Reagan and Bush administrations to tighten the economic blockade and discredit Cuban internationalism by attacking Cuba's human rights record on the handling of political dissidents. For example, Cuban representatives to the United Nations have attempted to gain support for a broader conception of national sovereignty that includes not only safeguarding territorial integrity but also guaranteeing respect for national identity and the right to self-determination (Alzugaray Treto 1991; D'Estéfano Pisani 1991). This conception of sovereignty is found in resolutions adopted by the U.N. General Assembly in November 1992 to end the U.S. embargo.

The Cuban leadership has achieved some limited success in garnering the support of several U.N. organizations in its attempt to overcome U.S. economic sanctions. For example, Cuba's unwavering support of the United Nations Educational, Scientific, and Cultural Organization (UNESCO), despite controversy surrounding its proposal (which led to the withdrawal from membership by the United States and Britian) in 1985 to create a new international news network more accessible to developing countries (Giffard 1989:195), may have prompted UNESCO to denounce Radio Martí in 1990 as a violation of Cuban sovereignty. Cuba has also cultivated a strong ally in the United Nations Food and Agriculture Organization (FAO) by offering to share its advances in the biotechnology of food production with needy Third World countries. The FAO has reciprocated recently by condemning the U.S. blockade of food to Cuba as a violation of human rights.

2

People's Courts: An Experiment in Legal Mobilization

One significant challenge confronting the leadership of a country embarked on the path of social development is to provide a basis for a common national experience. An essential precondition to regime support is that all citizens (including subsequent generations) can share in this process because it enables them to understand and accept the sacrifices required to achieve individual and national objectives. For precisely these reasons, participation in civic life serves as the common medium through which individuals can contribute and share in economic and political development (Fagen 1969:154–58).

Since the conditions of the Cuban revolution grew out of the guerrilla experience of struggle, discipline, and sacrifice, which only a few could share, Castro hit upon innovative ways to involve youth in comparable experiences. The most noteworthy featured the mobilization of youth in a nationwide campaign to increase literacy. While this tactic clearly served an ideological role in familiarizing the people with Marxism-Leninism and Castro's political objectives, it also gave youth an opportunity to have direct contact with and to develop empathy for the plight of the rural poor and the illiterate majority of the country. An enormous success (Kozol 1980; Leiner 1987; Wald 1978), the literacy campaign encouraged Castro to continue his efforts to tap the reservoir of commitment and sense of moral purpose that the revolution had aroused in its youth (Goodsell 1967:20).

Castro also undertook a major campaign in 1962 to create a system of popular justice that would help legitimate the nationalization of private property and support the fundamental redistribution of wealth. The People's Courts were controversial because they advanced a conception of the judicial role that would enlist the legal process as an educational tool for social change. Castro's desire to achieve substantive justice ruled out superficial procedural change. He wanted to create a set of revolutionary rights and duties that would force existing institutions to adapt to a new social reality. The system of popular justice complemented the literacy campaign because both were designed to provide the civic competence necessary for effective participation in social reconstruction. This chapter focuses principally on the role that the CDRs played in the administration of popular justice and examines why the experiment in People's Courts generally failed to realize its potential as a vehicle for social reconstruction.

The Politics of Socialist Legality

There were compelling historical reasons Cuban leaders felt a sense of urgency to undertake radical legal reforms. Cuba, like most other Latin American countries, does not have a strong constitutional tradition grounded in individual rights. According to Wiarda (1971), Latin American legal culture is based on "corporatism" and an organic conception of law and society. A general will based on group rights takes precedence over individualism. Consequently, the latifundio, or family-run agricultural enterprise, represented the lowest common denominator for the ascription of rights.

Judicial and administrative reforms based on principles of American jurisprudence were attempted during the U.S. occupation of Cuba from 1902 to 1909, but they failed to take hold because of the absence of indigenous support and opposition from U.S. corporate interests (Lockmiller 1937). It should be pointed out that the Cuban Supreme Court stood as an island of integrity in the sea of incompetence and graft characteristic of the lower courts. As Domínguez (1978:89, 99) notes, the Cuban Supreme Court frequently attacked undemocratic institutional practices only to have its rulings overturned by executive decree.

The so-called progressive urban reforms introduced by General Leonard Woods during the U.S. occupation at the turn of the century also ignored the plight of rural Cubans and the need to rectify the gross inequities in land use and ownership (Gillette 1973). A successful indigenous reform effort was mounted in 1940, culminating in the passage of a constitution involving far-reaching economic and social reforms. However, the promise of reform was quickly extinguished by the resumption of dictatorship, corruption, bureaucratic intransigence, and periodic U.S. intervention to repel any serious challenges to its hegemony in the region.

Not surprisingly, Castro, who was a lawyer by training, made it quite clear early in the revolution that the practice of law would be reorganized to serve socialist ends. For example, because of its open resistance to the provisional government, the Cuban Bar Association was soon taken over by Castro sympathizers, who expelled many of the members. Attorneys were thereafter assigned to work in law offices (*bufetes colectivos*) controlled by the government. Also, prosecutorial functions were substantially enlarged with the creation of the *fiscalia,* which handled ordinary crime and represented citizens' interests against official illegality (Evenson 1990:55–56). Perhaps in response to these changes and as a result of basic reorganization of legal education, attendance at law school dwindled from 2,853 in 1958–59 to 159 in 1971–72 (Salas 1979b:598). Most lawyers unsympathetic to the Castro regime anticipated these changes and were among the earliest wave of refugees and/or exiles.

Neither the Soviet Union nor China experienced a depletion of the same magnitude, which may account for an important difference in their legal reform processes. Juridical reform in these socialist countries was supplemented (if not overtaken by) purges and the use of terror to rid the legal profession of those unwilling to accommodate the ideological role orientations of a new order (Sharlet 1978). According to Hazard (1969), the Soviet popular courts were used initially as an instrument to redress the grievances the people had as a result of decades of abuse and indifference under the czar. This strategy harnessed the reservoir of resentment, rechanneling it into a flood of popular support (or acquiescence) ultimately involving coercion, repression, and political terror. In Cuba, by contrast, the object of resentment included not only the wealthy landowners and an oppressive dictator but also the entire U.S. colonial and imperialist apparatus, which reinforced feelings of inferiority by perpetuating economic dependency and social deprivation.

The Soviet legal intelligentsia led by the Paskuhunis school believed that because law was an instrument of private property, popular justice foreshadowed the end of law (Sharlet 1978:172). Stalin rejected this belief as naive and administratively nihilistic. He soon realized that law was indispensable for the maintenance of power in a new political order. However, the Cuban revolution faced a more daunting and perplexing task: how to generate support for an indigenous conception of a just society involving an open-ended, continual struggle of conscience against defeat by external aggression and internal self-doubt.

The literacy campaign and the experiment in popular justice involved complementary techniques to overcome these barriers to a just political order. The objective of the literacy campaign was to provide the skills to comprehend why the revolution was necessary. The system of popular justice was intended to increase awareness of how the goals and expectations of the revolution could be implemented through the observance and exercise of civic rights and duties. As Fagen (1969:12) observes, the strategy of mobilization combining pedagogical and juridical techniques paid a double dividend. Students and peasants could learn from each other. Students could experience the objective realities suggested by the avowedly political content of the civic training. Likewise, peasants could grasp how literacy would lift them from the bondage of dependency. Consequently, both peasant and student would increase their identification with the new order. The success of agrarian reform depended heavily on the effectiveness of the literacy campaign. The large-scale transfer of ownership rights and the redistribution of land held by the latifundios required that the peasants become more knowledgeable about efficient resource management.

Popular justice also helped weaken the counterrevolutionary actions that continued to be mounted after the insurrection. Peasants often were unknowingly enlisted in these activities, so a nonpunitive educational approach was necessary. Under these circumstances, equitable treatment was most likely if offenders were judged by their peers. Public involvement was encouraged to discuss the nature of the offenses and provide an opportunity to offer mitigating circumstances in the defendant's favor. A panel of lay judges elected by the people decided each case. Jurisdiction was limited to less serious felonies such as theft or vandalism and civil cases involving family matters such as divorce. In addition, the tribunals could rule on cases involving a precriminal state of dangerous behavior such as delinquency, loafing, or alcoholism. Penalties varied from public reprimand or fine to a period of detention involving productive labor. In all cases, the primary purpose was to "reeducate" the offender about conduct appropriate under socialism.

This format remained essentially the same until 1966 when the experiment was formalized and extended to encompass the major urban centers (Van der Plas 1987:127). During this time a number of significant changes were introduced that had the net effect of reducing popular control. The impetus for change appears to have stemmed from the increasing social turbulence caused by the introduction of moral incentives, deferred consumption, and reliance on volunteer labor to accelerate the processes of real economic growth. During this period Cuba experienced a sharp increase in absenteeism, crime, and delinquency (Kennedy 1973; Salas 1979b:103–18, 330–36); a shortage of housing and consumer goods (Hamberg 1986; Van der Plas 1987); and a rapidly expanding black market (Salas 1979b:66–76; 111–15). Consequently, by 1969, one year before the 10 million ton sugar harvest debacle, the Cuban leadership had already begun to reevaluate its strategies and techniques to bring about socialist development.

Implementing Neighborhood Justice

Although a complete explanation of why strategies of mobilization involving pedagogical and juridical techniques fell short of expectation is beyond the scope of this chapter, the attempt by the CDRs to use their control of popular courts to influence the distribution of goods and the administration of justice significantly undermined the democratic potential of these strategies. The CDRs were established in 1960 to provide a system of collective vigilance against invasion by the United States (Fagen 1969:69). Later, a system of surveillance and security was implemented in each neighborhood to monitor behavior and look out for sabotage and other attacks against the regime. As their membership grew, the CDRs were given responsibility for managing a larger number of tasks and services related to the goal of integrating the whole population into the revolutionary process. These activities generally included the protection of public health, public order, and safety and the distribution of rationed goods and services (Domínguez 1978:64; Fagen 1969:80).

The CDRs also served until 1966 as a liaison between management and employees by providing alternative employment for workers idled by shortages or needed to complete public works or housing projects. When fifty-five thousand small businesses and restaurants were nationalized in 1968, supervisory tasks were handed over to inspectors picked from the CDR membership (Van der Plas 1987:100). As a consequence of these activities, CDR members acquired leadership of key administrative posts through local elections (*poder local*), seemingly guaranteeing dominance in local governance until the Cuban leadership curiously decided against institutionalizing local governance in this form (Van der Plas 1987:100).

In a state redistributive economy plagued by persistent shortages, the potential for corruption or abuse is high among those who serve as intermediaries in the chain of distribution. Delegated authority and discretion go hand in hand, increasing the opportunity for deviation from official norms and regulations. Castro and Cuban officials first became aware in 1962 of the existence of a secret network (the true proportions of which were unknown) run by a faction of party members led by Anabal Escalante. The Escalante "microfaction," as Castro called it, consisted of old-line prerevolutionary communists opposed to Guevara's program for radical economic reform. As secretary of the Integrated Revolutionary Organizations (ORI, a precursor to the Cuban Communist Party), Escalante controlled a network of national and provincial officials who owed their allegiance to him, giving him enormous leverage over the implementation of policies he opposed. His tactics included fanning the fire of disenchantment with Guevara's extremism that was smoldering among senior Soviet officials and technicians.

After sending Escalante away on an extended diplomatic mission to Czechoslovakia, Castro described in some detail how the network was constructed and operated in a speech on "bureaucracy and sectarianism." The "nuclei" of trusted associates, as Castro (1983b:48, 56–59) called them, functioned through a system of selective recruitment, patronage, and bribes, circumventing ministry policies. To denigrate this network, Castro (1983b:61–62) intimated that most had previous ties to the *mujalistas*, or union leaders who had collaborated with Batista during the 1950s. Castro's subsequent purge led to the expulsion of a significant percentage of party members in the provinces, approximately one-third of whom had obtained their membership through election as "exemplary workers" (Domínguez 1978:213–14). Although nearly one-half of the estimated fifteen thousand ORI members were expelled, a significant number of members retained their positions in the reconstituted party, according to Domínguez (1978:217), and therefore still carried the "Escalante taint."

As subsequent purges in 1966 and 1968 indicate, the Cuban leadership had seriously underestimated the true dimensions of the network beyond the provincial level. The leadership of the Confederation of Cuban Labor (CTC) came under suspicion when connections were traced among several CTC officials; José Matar, national director of the CDRs; and Escalante associates. The pervasiveness of the Escalante faction called into question the appropriateness of maintaining functional ties between the CDR leadership and labor. Consequently, the authority the CDRs possessed as employment intermediaries was ended, resulting in the expulsion of 17 percent of their membership (Domínguez 1978:263). Similarly, nearly one-half of the national directorate was replaced, and efforts were made to professionalize cadres in provincial and local leadership positions (Domínguez 1978:266).

The vast majority of members of these organizations, however, are neither party members nor exemplary workers. Their ability to cope in an economy of scarcity depends primarily on the strength of connections between their relatives and friends. Network intermediaries must be capable of functioning in this uncertain and risky environment in order to expedite the transfer of goods and services to those at the very terminus of the chain of distribution (Burt and Minor 1983). Effectiveness at this level therefore depends less on party connections or subgroup cohesiveness than on the possibility of forming instrumental and temporary relationships based on either trust or expediency. Not surprisingly, Castro lamented the fact that his purge of the CDRs had done little to thwart the rise of a new group of intermediaries within unofficial networks of exchange (Van der Plas 1987:97–98).

Evidence documenting the persistence of these networks is largely limited to anecdotal information such as that provided to Lewis (1977a; 1977b) by informants to his intriguing oral history of the first decade of the Cuban revolution. In one particularly poignant narrative, Inocencia and her husband, Reinaldo, recounted their turbulent and difficult years serving as coordinators of the local CDR in Havana, whose leadership was compromised by pervasive corruption. They took great pride in relating how they had effectively organized and recruited members to assist in early public health campaigns and a census that required enormous energy and perseverance. But they also expressed their disgust and resentment at having to take orders from "paid functionaries" who ran district offices of the CDRs (Lewis 1977b:382). Inocencia vividly described the almost endless forms that corruption assumed under the guise of official discretion and that implicated almost everyone in the community. She also recounted the utter frustration and anger she experienced when the CDR leaders she courageously exposed for corruption, resulting in the loss of her CDR position, were promoted, rather than punished, for their misbehavior (Lewis 1977b:385–87).

The experiment in popular justice was expected to root out individuals who organized or participated in these illegal exchange networks. Popular courts were initially placed under the control of the Ministry of Justice, where lawyers still exercised some influence. Soon, however, the courts were put under a national directorate accountable to the head of mass organizations. The courts exercised jurisdiction over civil conflicts as well as over some criminal offenses that fell broadly within the definition of antisocial conduct. Charges could be brought by private citizens, the CDR, the police, and even members of the court. Although no data are available to establish the frequency with which cases reached the courts through these various avenues, it is evident that the CDRs were capable of generating a substantial number of cases in the performance of their vigilance functions (Salas 1979b:306–12). There were almost no guidelines for the preparation of cases, and quite frequently complaints lacked specific charges. This state of affairs continued until an official manual was adopted delineating rights of the accused, crimes, charging processes, and the range of sanctions (Berman 1969:1344–45; Salas 1983: 591).

Defining a New Role for the CDR

A recurrent criticism leveled at the CDR, which ultimately led to a considerable contraction of its myriad roles after 1969, was its general ineffectiveness in performing vigilance functions. Property crimes, especially theft of state property, rose sharply from a low of 6.55 percent in 1964 to 33 percent in 1969 (Van der Plas 1987:106). Salas (1979b:107) reports that in 1967 juveniles (or adults working with juveniles) accounted for 27 percent of all thefts. Cuban officials attributed this increase to long absences of residents from homes and to work sites left unattended during periods of voluntary labor. Although these environmental factors were significant, the conflicting roles of CDR members in the administration of popular justice and the distribution of goods may have exacerbated the crime problem by compromising the judicial process.

First, CDR members exerted an enormous influence over the recruitment and selection of lay judges, ensuring the election of a large percentage of CDR members to these posts. Formal guidelines and procedures were minimal, giving wide latitude in fact gathering, case disposition, and sentencing (Berman 1969:1321–26). Wide disparities in case dispositions were minimized, however, because most sentences involved admonishment or reeducation rather than imprisonment. Nevertheless, popular courts were criticized for leniency and lack of objective data, such as the prior criminal records needed to identify repeat criminal activity (Salas 1979b:215). During a three-month period in 1969, for example, police reported that 83 percent of all persons arrested were recidivists (Salas 1979b:116).

Second, CDR members played an important role in determining who would be exonerated of wrongdoing by attesting to the "moral surety" of the defendant. Technically, CDR members could serve as a character reference only if the case would not bring "disrepute to the CDR," thus concealing the potential involvement of other members in the crime (Salas 1979b:315). Although technically the lay defense had to come from a zone other than that in which the defendant resided, defendants who were CDR members could be defended by members from the same local chapter if there were mitigating factors favoring acquittal. This practice, which ended in 1977, served in some instances to protect CDR activities from further investigation (Van der Plas 1987:110–11). Furthermore, a nearly exclusive emphasis on the arrest of consumers, rather than sellers of black market goods, may have unintentionally reinforced network ties by enabling unscrupulous CDR leaders to avoid prosecution (Salas 1979b:76).

As Salazar, another informant in the Lewis (1977a) study, pointed out, corrupt CDR leaders such as José Dávalos compromised the integrity of popular justice by diverting from prosecution persons whose knowledge of criminal activity jeopardized Dávalos's position. Dávalos was voted the local CDR coordinator even though most people in the neighborhood were aware of his running an illegal workshop out of his home. Salazar speculated that Dávalos was kept in office because "they knew Dávalos wouldn't interfere with the gambling and a lot of other things that go on in the barrio" (Lewis 1977a:397). When a bus driver was arrested in Dávalos's district for stealing fares, he was found not guilty largely because Dávalos testified on behalf of his character, saying that he was not "a thief by nature." When the case was subsequently investigated by the Technical Department, Dávalos covered up the fact that the driver had previously stolen fares and that he did not reside in the district.

When Salazar attempted to tell the truth about the incident, he was rebuffed.

Third, CDR members were vested with the authority to supervise and rehabilitate offenders while in confinement and, once released, to reintegrate them back into society. This supervisory parole function brought about a coordinated approach to community corrections involving more than seven thousand activists by 1975. A primary drawback of combining parole and law enforcement functions, as Salas (1979b:323) perceptively notes, was that it blurred the line between vigilance and vigilantism, perpetuating, rather than dissolving, the network linking perpetrator and accuser in a pattern of criminal recidivism. Since the mid-1970s, however, many supervisory functions have been taken over by professionals, considerably reducing the potential for role conflict and limiting the CDRs to the task of crime detection and social prevention.

The transition to a prevention mission occurred as a result of criticisms voiced during the Forum for Internal Order in 1969. The CDRs were criticized for failing to generate detailed and useful information about the source, incidence, and patterns of criminal activity. Forum participants recommended that CDR members develop new techniques of investigation to assist police in the detection and prevention of crime. Toward this end, the National Front for Social Prevention was created to train members in new prevention and rehabilitation techniques. This change in mandate was accompanied by the transfer of jurisdiction of cases involving judgments about social dangerousness (e.g., theft of state property, embezzlement, and black market activities) from popular courts to regular municipal and provisional courts (Van der Plas 1987:136). Also, the CDRs were asked to conduct education campaigns to increase awareness among families, neighborhoods, and schools about the special needs of problem youth and to recruit volunteers to assist professionals in the rehabilitation of delinquent youth.

Beyond these educational campaigns, however, the main thrust of CDR reforms involved strengthening its surveillance and security capabilities in law enforcement. For example, neighborhoods and communities were subdivided into zones to facilitate the collection of systematic data on criminal behavior (Salas 1979b:307–8). Whenever possible, offenders are now debriefed by means of *actos de repudio* (repudiation meetings), which gather details about the modus operandi and other factors bearing on the commission of the crime. In addition, the offender is given an opportunity to "reply" in exchange for leniency by answering questions pertaining to weaknesses in security exploited in the commission of the crime that could be eliminated in the future (Salas 1979b:313–14; Van der Plas 1987:284–85).

Since the commencement of a "special period" in Cuba, the CDRs' functions have been further reorganized under the new leadership of General Sixto Batista, appointed by Castro in February 1990. General Batista has begun to streamline the CDRs by eliminating intermediate administrative layers and intensifying crime-control activities. In addition, the CDRs will be assisting in the relocation of surplus personnel idled or displaced by shortage-related shutdowns of their work centers (FBIS 1991b). The restructuring of the CDRs was preceded by Castro's October 1990 announcement (Granma Weekly Review 1990a) of the creation of People's Councils in the city of Havana.

The ninety-three People's Councils consist of a president elected by delegates of the Organs of People Power (OPP) (discussed in Chapter 5) and staff to coordinate the detection of illicit activities conducted by small businesses and restaurants in more than fifteen hundred districts. The councils are staffed by CDR members, police, and other personnel from the Ministry of the Interior. The presidents of the People's Councils, established by the Council of State, report directly to Castro, who meets with them on a regular basis (FBIS 1990g:2). At their first meeting, Castro underscored their high educational attainment and extensive professional experience. Significantly, the People's Councils will coordinate their work with various ongoing task forces created by the minister of justice, such as Operation Cascabel (FBIS 1991d) and Maceta (FBIS 1991e), to interdict in embezzlement and bribery. Thus, the Cuban leadership has redoubled its efforts to unravel the complex network of ties that support the extensive black market in goods and services that persists despite years of concerted action.

Assessing the Experiment in People's Courts

Significantly, the experiment in People's Courts was phased out by the early 1970s, and a process of relegalization was begun that culminated in major judicial reorganization in 1973, 1977, and 1979 and thereby returned control of the judiciary to legal professionals (Azicri 1988:108–10; Irons 1981; Salas 1979b:221–23). Only two features of popular courts have survived these subsequent reforms: Lay judges continue to sit on municipal and provincial tribunals, and lower-court judges remain administratively accountable to local delegates of the OPP. The judicial system in Cuba today differs fundamentally in most other respects from its populist predecessor. For example, trial court judges are substantively accountable for their decisions to the National Assembly and the Council of State. Trial proceedings are now handled by a permanent prosecutor (since 1977), procedural rules have become more complex, and defendants may obtain an attorney. CDR participation has been limited since 1979 to providing the equivalent of a presentence report to the judge (Van der Plas 1987:288).

In addition to these changes, the jurisdiction of municipal tribunals was considerably expanded in 1977, partly because many economic crimes previously treated as misdemeanors were upgraded. This has contributed to dramatic change in the types of cases tried. For example, the majority of cases handled by popular courts included the damage and theft of private property. Today, the bulk of the caseload of a municipal court involves theft of state property and other crimes against the state (Van der Plas 1987:279–80).

Information remains fragmentary and incomplete as to why this experiment was discontinued in its original form. Castro and other policymakers did not make their intentions very clear when introducing the People's Courts in 1962. It was not until 1966 that Central Committee member Blas Roca Calderío officially characterized people's justice as the attempt "to edify and consolidate the new society of socialism and communism, to educate the new man, . . . and to secure and to perfect the rules of socialist communism" (Berman 1969:1318). This ambiguity was matched by placing lay jurists under the administrative jurisdiction of existing courts, which invited duplication and conflict (Salas 1983:603). Clearly, as Berman and Whiting (1980:477–78) report, the legal profession, particularly jurists, bitterly opposed this foray into nonprofessionalism. They underscored the many weaknesses and inconsistencies of a judicial system lacking in professional standards, common formal procedures, sentences, sanctions, and the like. Moreover, the failure of the People's Courts to develop effective working relationships with police contributed to a dramatic decline in caseload over time, further questioning the need for their existence (Salas 1983:608).

Experiments in popular justice in China, for example, were undermined largely because they had become an instrument for political repression during the Cultural Revolution. Mao Zedong skillfully directed the Red Guard's campaign of fear and retribution at technocrats and intellectuals who had become indifferent to the mass line (Yang 1989). Some legal observers, such as Brady (1982), argue that, although regrettable, these tactics were necessary to rejuvenate the populist and equalitarian underpinnings of the socialist revolution. In contrast, Lewis (1986) and Turk (1989) contend that the Cultural Revolution reflected a factional power struggle in which popular courts served as a convenient tool for Mao to disable political rivals. In any event, a new period of legal reform was launched by Deng Xiaoping in 1982 to support the adoption of decentralized economic structures governed by the principles of competitive capitalism. Even though these reforms promote professionalization, they do not provide a meaningful framework to handle problems of equity and rights that are likely to become more acute as modernization proceeds (Brady 1982).

Azicri (1985:309) contends that the early period of induced legal change through the People's Courts was followed by a period of legal reorganization that "reinforced" social changes achieved through these initial experiments. Azicri (1985:317) also claims that popular courts were instrumental in popularizing the revolution's conception of equality and justice and that this enabled revolutionary culture to play a "decisive role in legitimizing legal and judicial institutions that emerged in subsequent years." The difficulty with Azicri's plausible account is that he may be forcing the processes of legal reform to fit into a theory of socialist development that has not consistently guided the processes of institutionalization. Moreover, there is little evidence that the most significant representatives of socialist law, such as the Family Code and the Code on Children and Youth (see Chapter 4), grew out of experience with the People's Courts.

Guevara and Castro reversed the sequence of socialist development. They used legal institutions to stimulate awareness and generate support for incipient economic structures and internationalist relationships that were fragile and precarious at that time. Popular courts were expected to generate a social conscience from feelings of shame or indignity suffered for behavior associated with the consumption orientation of capitalist institutions. This approach was inconsistent with Castro's belief that *conciencia* derived from feelings of compassion and the motivation to rectify injustice, not atone for error. Although this focus on shame may have increased consciousness of the evils of international capitalism, it provided little guidance as to the kind of behavior that was considered acceptable. In this respect, courts faced institutional barriers that prevented them from enunciating or prescribing specific policies to achieve social objectives (Baum 1981; Horowitz 1977). Courts depended on a diverse number of secondary populations (i.e., officials, administrators, and target groups), all of whom contributed to the interpretation and implementation of judicial rulings (Johnson and Canon 1984). No clear and consistent doctrine emerged from those involved in Cuban popular justice. The use of labor courts and other administrative devices to regulate the workplace illustrated the limited reach of courts and underscored the necessity for other secondary populations to be continually involved in enforcement activities.

Another deficiency in Cuban popular justice is that it greatly exaggerated the possibility of changing prerevolutionary behavior and values. Political corruption and inequality were pervasive in prerevolutionary Cuba. The bold steps to rectify the maldistribution of social goods were implemented with little controversy because they enjoyed popular support. However, the willingness to accept a reduction in consumer goods for social betterment was not sufficiently entrenched to displace systems of exchange that short-circuited the connection between social contribution and reward. In this regard, as Scheingold (1974:212) concludes, "legal tactics are likely to work best in connection with relatively severe deprivations and among groups which are reasonably well socialized. . . . The obstacles are more serious with alienated subcultures." Careful observers of Cuban law support Azicri's (1981:59) conclusion: "The Popular Courts were mainly for the well integrated, not for marginal or alienated citizens." Cuban courts were not really adjudicating cases to redress injustices; they were punishing behavior opposed to a new order that was neither shared nor comprehended by all people.

3

Reorganizing Labor: Moral Incentives and Discipline

Analyses of Cuban social development frequently become sidetracked into esoteric debates about economic performance and the feasibility of achieving equity with growth. To be sure, as the previous chapter suggests, Cuban leaders believed that production and distribution had to be guided by considerations of social equity and justice. But *conciencia*, as Castro and Guevara construed the term, involved a conception of the virtuous human conduct needed to achieve a just society rather than a definitive principle to guide economic growth. Therefore, much of the ongoing debate regarding the advisability and feasibility of Cuba adopting or rejecting market mechanisms seems misplaced. The ethic of sacrifice and the logic of struggle were concerned with making the heroic virtues of courageous leadership, unflinching risk-taking, improvisation, and self-denial intrinsic to human nature. Material or moral incentives and rewards were considered only temporary tactics in a much deeper and longer struggle to free socialist people from exploitative relationships, which were embedded in feelings of insecurity and inadequacy and were reinforced by inequality, materialism, and greed.

The inconsistent and sometimes paradoxical consequences of Cuban economic policies over time can be explained in part by the continual and sometimes convoluted struggle to overcome the subjective conditions that block processes of social transformation. This does not downplay the importance of other factors shaping Cuba's socialist accumulation strategies but merely suggests that self-interest limits the capacity to pursue economic goals of productivity, growth, and social justice simultaneously and consistently. The attempt, for example, to adopt a long-term accumulation strategy for diversification requires that consumption be forgone in favor of investment. Exchange networks, however, divert currency and resources from planned to unplanned uses. Networks also have a symbolic impact. They undermine legitimate state control over the normative system of rewards and sanctions by providing an alternative mechanism through which claims to the possession of scarce resources, goods, and social status can be redeemed.

Significantly, the success of Cuban policies for economic growth has largely turned upon the leadership's ability to control the social and psychological processes of work, where merit is rewarded with recognition, esteem, status, and prestige. In the first two decades of the revolution, improvements in productivity were sought through exhortation and moral appeals involving emulation, technical norms, and juridical sanctions. Since the early 1980s, however, the tactics have become more sophisticated, drawing on psychological techniques and technological experimentation to identify the optimum conditions in which individual moral growth and economic productivity can occur simultaneously and harmoniously. This chapter describes how work was reorganized around moral incentives; examines the roles workers, unions, management, and the FMC played in advancing or impeding economic and social objectives; and assesses the dilemmas that alternative work structures such as microbrigades pose for striking an effective balance between economic growth and respect for individual rights.

Emulation and Wage Reform

In the first decade of the revolution, Cuban policymakers had to fulfill their pledge quickly to bring about an egalitarian redistribution of wealth and income and to undertake a massive investment in social goods such as health care, education, and welfare services. The former objective entailed the extensive nationalization of enterprises, the reorganization of agriculture, and, importantly, the restructuring of labor, which caused extensive social dislocation and hardship. Soviet aid, loans, and the purchase of sugar on favorable terms, along with eventual trade with Eastern Europe, helped offset the adverse effects of the U.S. blockade and eased the strain involved in reallocating resources to social investments rather than to the production of consumer goods. After the tumultuous 1960s, Cuban policymakers drew on centralized and decentralized planning models, employing mixed incentive systems to sustain intermittent periods of modest economic growth and social stability until the mid-1980s, when economic performance declined and social conflict and dissidence increased.

Economists differ on how to interpret the role of nonmaterial incentives in the changes in Cuban economic performance. Mesa-Lago (1968; 1978) attributes Cuba's poor economic performance in the late 1960s and early 1970s, as well as its recent economic difficulties during the period of rectification after 1985, to the mistaken belief that workers could be motivated to produce through nonmaterial incentives. In contrast, Zimbalist and Eckstein (1987:10) conclude that "given the extensive goods short-ages at the time engendered by the accumulation strategy and adherence to equalitarian norms, there was no choice but to rely on nonmaterial incentives to motivate work." The authors also speculate, however, that this choice may have been a conscious one since it theoretically enabled Cuba to handle its foreign debt and pursue investment in capital goods by forcing domestic savings.

There is no question that Cuban leaders recognize the critical importance of carefully planned investment in sustaining economic growth. However, the attempt to alter the ratio between production and consumption requires more than just controlling the volume of savings. Rather, it necessitates the effective interdiction and control of the mechanisms of supply and demand through which money and goods are exchanged. A significant but unknown proportion of economic activity in Cuba occurs beyond the reach of planners, distorting production processes and undermining distributional equity.

Nonmaterial incentives were introduced, in part, to weaken money and goods as bases of status and prestige. Voluntary work was intended to effectuate feelings of equal self-worth by bringing people together to complete projects that contributed to the common good. Guevara (1968d:337–38) believed that if each worker adopted a selfless attitude and gave overriding priority to the completion of projects regardless of the specific tasks assigned to any one individual, then the value of total output could be measured in terms of the contribution each worker made to social development as a whole. Wages and compensation would not be governed solely by age, experience, or political favoritism but also by a willingness to conserve and protect state property and to contribute voluntary time to projects benefiting the public good.

Unfortunately, the system of emulation was used as a lever by planners to iron out prerevolutionary inequalities in the wage structure, a task this system was ill-suited to perform. A new wage structure could not be imposed all at once without risking the alienation of skilled workers, so adjustments had to be made incrementally. Consequently, workers with wages above the new scales could continue to draw their old wages or salaries with the caveat that 25 percent of the total amount, or *en plus,* was a gift of the revolution (Zimbalist and Brundenius 1989:122). This allowed the phasing out of wage differences through retirement of older workers. In many instances, however, the *en plus* system was used to obligate workers to work longer hours or overfill quotas to justify their total wages (Mesa-Lago 1968:105). Moreover, work-center agreements were so general that managers had wide latitude in the interpretation and implementation of compensation schedules (Mesa-Lago 1968:178–79). Individual emulation contracts included multiple criteria by which a worker's contribution could be evaluated, such as punctuality, cooperativeness, minimization of absenteeism or wastefulness, overfulfillment of output quotas, and quality control. Consequently, workers could never be certain of the exact basis on which their wages or prices were calculated.

Perhaps the most persuasive evidence that socialist emulation was undermined by faulty planning was the systematic and pervasive absenteeism in the late 1960s plaguing almost every work center. In the absence of a system of uniform norms to measure output, workers were paid the same wages no matter how much they produced. This contributed to a substantial increase in consumer liquidity unmatched by a proportionate increase in productivity. In essence, the money in circulation far exceeded the supply of available goods. Under these conditions there was little incentive to work. By 1970 an estimated 20 to 30 percent of workers were absent on any given day (Domínguez 1978:275). This prompted Castro (1983d:113) to complain that rising absenteeism posed "one of the most urgent battles" facing the regime. Castro (1983d:124) threatened retaliation by depriving repeat offenders of access to goods and services and by suspending pay. He was soon convinced, however, that the magnitude of the problem required a systematic and punitive juridical response.

Work-Center Accountability:
Indiscipline, Absenteeism, and Sociolismo

Grievance commissions existed to handle work-related disputes in enterprise work centers as early as 1961. These commissions were responsible for enforcing regulations against lateness, absenteeism, work stoppages, and other behavior affecting worker discipline and productivity. They relied primarily on educational strategies to increase consciousness of revolutionary crimes and instill a respect for state property. Castro soon became critical of these commissions (which operated essentially like People's Courts) because of their laxity, noting that "many members . . . seem to be on the side of absenteeism and vagrancy" (Salas 1979b:337).

Subsequent revisions were made in 1965 to formalize procedures and to stiffen penalties, but these did little to stem the tide of labor indiscipline and low productivity. Consequently, in 1971 a law against loafing was passed, further stiffening penalties. This law had three aims: to identify nonworkers and integrate them into the work force, to identify those who had deserted work, and to punish those who were chronically absent from work (Kennedy 1973:1198–1201). The law also transferred penal jurisdiction from the traditional courts to the Labor Courts. Interestingly, employers reacted negatively to this development and usually refused to surrender their workers to forums over which they exercised little influence and control. In response, the vast majority of the disciplinary cases were handled informally by factory labor councils in which workers were usually admonished, rather than punished, for their misbehavior (Salas 1979b:347–48).

The Ley Contra la Vagrancia (Law Against Loafing) was significant because it marked a convergence of criminological and economic thinking about factors contributing to low productivity. Cuban leaders' confidence in centralized control of production through JUCEPLAN (Cuba's central economic planning organization until 1974) was shaken by the widening disparity between production forecasts and local capabilities (Zimbalist and Eckstein 1987:11–12; Pérez-López 1987). This not only pointed to basic defects in central resource allocation but also suggested mismanagement and the misuse of available labor. Criminologists blamed problems of production on management leniency and corruption. They also found that as absenteeism increased, so did vagrancy, which, in turn, was strongly associated with crime and delinquency. Although absenteeism and vagrancy were not in themselves crimes, they served as breeding grounds for other forms of delinquent and criminal behavior (Salas 1979b:360). Thus, the 1971 law was not merely designed to concentrate on those with bad work habits but also to single out the *vago respetuoso*, i.e., the loafer who was tolerated by family and friends. Consequently, the real target of the antiloafing law was not so much the offender's behavior as it was the breakup of the network of mutual protection (or *sociolismo*) that perpetuated such behavior.

The creation of a system for the adjudication of labor problems stemmed largely from the pressures for increased productivity that the Cuban regime began to experience in the early 1970s. The System of Economic Management and Planning (SDPE) and the Organs of People Power (national and subnational legislative assemblies) were introduced in 1974 and 1976, respectively, to provide a system of accountability and control within which to achieve national economic and social goals (Zimbalist and Brundenius 1989:124–25). The SDPE considerably decentralized economic planning by giving enterprises primary responsibility for cost accounting. Likewise, the OPP, consisting of elected delegates, increased local supervision over the delivery of essential public and social services, such as transportation, schools, and polyclinics.

Beginning in 1974, work norms were set for each enterprise and service entity, such as hospitals, schools, and clinics. These norms consist of systems of accounting in which production or performance schedules are set according to the level of capability reflected by the skills workers have in each enterprise or work center (Pérez-Stable 1986). This enables the Ministry of Labor to allocate labor according to projected output. As of 1986 norms had been set for approximately one-half of the work force, but that number had probably grown considerably larger by the early 1990s (Fitzgerald 1990b:117–20).

Ironically, this system of work-center accountability and labor discipline has provoked forms of adaptation and resistance that work against the most productive use of human resources, such as well-educated and highly skilled technical and professional workers. As Fitzgerald (1989; 1990b:49–51) reports, enterprise and work-center managers have developed creative ways to cope with the pressures they face to retain intermediate-level cadres threatened by displacement by younger, better-educated professionals. These managers, consisting largely of "old cadres" (those who owe their positions to participation in the insurrection) are put in a bind. In order to retain older experienced workers, who may elect to take better jobs, a number of incentives must be provided to keep them around. Unable to offer direct-pay inducements, managers resort to "buddyism" and many other technically illegal tactics, such as reduced hours, extended vacations, better housing, promises of job security and promotions, falsification of work sheets, and exaggerated output. This ensures loyalty of the worker to the manager and amounts to a mutual protection racket. Under these conditions, there is little incentive or need to hire better-skilled but inexperienced younger workers, who consequently are forced to take jobs in which they are underemployed and their skills underused.

Older cadres resist attempts to increase participation in work-center decisionmaking because of fear of exposure. This has the unfortunate effect of reinforcing a vicious cycle between "malign" interference by enterprise managers and "benign" or paternalistic intervention by Castro or other central bureaucrats to resolve bottlenecks in production processes (Fitzgerald 1989:287). Fitzgerald (1990b:113) reports, for example, that Castro deploys a personal staff of twenty *compañeros* (discussed in Chapter 5) for troubleshooting and coordination. Although they may solve an immediate problem, the planning process is disrupted, sometimes creating expectations that cannot be fulfilled.

Castro's disenchantment with the managerial abuses of decentralization under SDPE was reinforced by disgust with the capitalist excesses of the free farmers' market introduced in the early 1980s. Despite some limited evidence of its positive impact on overall economic growth, the farmers' market spawned the dramatic growth of an entrepreneurial class, which Castro believed threatened to undermine the preeminence of moral incentives. Independent farmers were accused of accumulating fortunes, while truckers, vendors, restaurant managers, and enterprise managers were condemned for profiting as intermediaries in the transfer and sale of produce and other goods (Zimbalist and Brundenius 1989:138;

Mesa-Lago 1989:102). Particularly galling to Castro was the use of work time and state resources for personal enrichment.

A recent longitudinal study of the collectivization and privatization of agriculture in Hungary during the communist and postcommunist period suggests that Castro's fears may have been well founded. Szeleyni (1988:213–15) found that independent, family-based farmers successfully resisted collectivization by setting up a network through which they sold their produce and other goods. The wealth and entrepreneurial skills acquired during the years of communist control enabled these farmers to effectively exploit the limited opportunities afforded by economic liberalization in the 1980s and to translate this into political power in the subsequent period of waning communist control.

By 1986 the free farmers' markets had been discontinued. Cuban leaders began to deliberate on ways to restructure state financing in order to minimize management-related abuses (Mesa-Lago 1989). The 1979 Penal Code (see Azicri 1980a) was amended in 1988 to expand the list of administrative crimes against the state to include speculation, hoarding, deception of consumers, and damage to economic plans.

Increased economic growth during this period of liberalization had a mixed impact on overall economic performance. From 1980 to 1985 rapid economic growth was led by expansion of capital goods production in farm machinery, electronics, and prefabricated materials (Zimbalist and Brundenius 1989:30, 84–90). Nevertheless, Mesa-Lago (1989) reports that the state budget deficit increased by 279 percent in 1987, suggesting that Cuba was living beyond its means during 1980 to 1985 and that extended growth increased debt and other macro imbalances, which were subsequently paid for. State subsidies for food and other subsistence items were increased in order to offset market-driven price increases, and some enterprises may have increased state budget support to cover revenue shortfalls caused by the diversion of their resources into private-market activities.

Union Democratization and Rectification

Castro's displeasure at these many abuses led to the adoption of a policy for the rectification of errors at the Third Party Congress in 1986. At that time, Castro acknowledged that the causes of these problems were varied and that no universal formula of discipline existed that could be appropriately and consistently applied to each work center. Instead, Castro (Granma Weekly Review 1986c) stressed that he was searching for a "special discipline" with standards and techniques appropriate to the special needs and functions of hospitals, schools, and all other Cuban institutions involved in national economic performance. In a scenario reminiscent of Foucault's disciplinary society of normalization, Castro indicated that more specific expectations, standards of competence and performance, and sanctions and punishment could be devised to deal with the forms of work misbehavior involving negligence, underperformance, or incompetence.

For example, Decree Law 113 (1989) was promulgated to establish national and provincial panels of physicians and health professionals to regulate professional conduct in the public health sector. A considerable number of regulations pertain to offenses involving falsification of medical diagnoses for unexcused absences or other illegal purposes, overreliance on paramedical technicians, and failure to provide all services to patients in a competent and respectful manner. Nevertheless, on the whole the regulations establish rigorous and uniform standards aimed at improving the quality of health care provided to the Cuban people.

Castro also urged that if workers developed more "demanding attitudes" of each other, then indiscipline among the minority would decrease (Granma Weekly Review 1986c). The judicialization of work and, more recently, the professionalization of the response to delinquency signaled a growing disenchantment among Cuban leaders with their inability to direct the pace of economic performance without adopting more comprehensive methods of discipline to control the processes of social development. This is not to say that law fades away or that respect for individual rights disappears but that behavioral norms are simply incorporated into a whole continuum of apparatuses (e.g., medical, educational, and scientific) that perform regulatory functions. Consequently, discourse about individual rights is increasingly recast into a science of norms about acceptable individual behavior and professional conduct. For example, Cuban psychologists (see Part 3) have conducted several experimental studies to identify the personality and social factors that motivate individuals to become professionals, to discover the nature of beliefs and value orientations they acquire, and to determine how these variables influence and shape their attitudes and professional judgment.

Castro's reluctance to support a more independent labor movement was rooted in his well-founded suspicion that the *mujalista*-dominated labor leadership had counterrevolutionary tendencies. Nearly all the leaders of the Confederation of Cuban Labor came under suspicion because they had been supporters or sympathizers of *mujalismo*. (Eusebio Mujal, who headed the CTC during the 1940s and 1950s, collaborated with the Batista dictatorship against the insurrection in return for government support of union policies.) More than two-thirds of this group publicly pledged to support private property and opposed communism (Fuller 1985:162–64). Many of these leaders had been expelled by

1960, including those who had participated in the 26 of July Movement (Alvaréz Díaz et al. 1963:115). Even though this may have dampened overt political opposition, it did little to deter the formation under Escalante's leadership of an extensive network of privilege and influence lubricated by bribes and illicit exchanges.

It became increasingly clear to Castro that poor economic performance was due to ineptness and collusion between management and union leaders (Castro 1983d:128, 130). Castro (1983d:119; 1983e:139) accused the vanguard workers promoted by Escalante's associates of elitism and corruption and rejected their moral authority to lead the rank and file. Free union elections could help root out these corrupt elements, facilitating their replacement by party cadres unburdened by divided loyalties between prerevolutionary *mujalistas* and the revolutionary leadership. Castro (1983d:131) believed that this strategy would expand party membership among workers, thus increasing the party's ability to truly represent workers' interests and concerns in policymaking processes. A strong party presence in union governance was also considered crucial to long-term viability of party leadership at a time when it was contemplating a withdrawal from a direct role in administrative functions (Fuller 1985:200–6).

The two most significant methods used to democratize unions have been elections and grievance or dispute resolution processes. Cuban scholars such as Mesa-Lago (1978) and Domínguez (1978) were generally critical of the adequacy of union representation. They were convinced that because elections were essentially indirect and noncompetitive, party-dominated affairs, workers and their representatives had almost no impact on work-center planning processes. However, Fuller's (1992) more recent study demonstrates that union members and their representatives have acquired greater influence over workplace conditions and the planning cycle than before. Moreover, unions have achieved some degree of independence from management in performing a *contrapardita* role by contributing to the evaluation of sector plans. Participation in intermediate levels of planning processes ensures influence over the implementation and impact of resource allocation at the work site. Grievance processes also provide union representatives an opportunity, if they choose, to question management abuses and irregularities in personnel decisions that may result in the prejudicial removal of workers (Fuller 1985:423–24).

An important event marking the ascendancy of union influence was the assumption of control over grievance processes by the CTC in 1977. Fuller (1992) contends that the three years in which the CTC administered labor councils marked a watershed for workers' rights. Through their union representatives, workers challenged a variety of management decisions, including discrimination in hiring and promotions, transfers, and terminations. Workers sought a more vigorous and informed defense of their rights, expecting their union representatives "to function as lawyers of sorts" (Fuller 1992:191). Interestingly, a significant proportion of the cases involved disputes over remuneration and transfers. Management interference and noncompliance occurred most frequently in these cases because they directly impinged on management prerogatives essential to the maintenance of network control. In this regard, as the Yugoslavian experience with workers' courts attests, workers are more likely to bring their cases to courts that provide legal counsel, are governed by formal procedures, and compensate the workers for management wrongdoing (Hayden 1985:323–26)

The FMC appears to have provided an important stimulus to a more aggressive union defense of workers' rights. In 1971 the FMC created a secretariat within the CTC to advocate for women's rights in the workplace. The Feminine Front (now called the Department of Women's Affairs) attempted to rectify women's underrepresentation in the work force by eliminating discrimination in the workplace (Evenson 1986b). After achieving significant gains in the 1970s for women, FMC leaders reacted with foreboding to decentralization of enterprise management under the SDPE because they feared that this might erode employment gains achieved during the early 1970s. Their fears were well founded. Management used efficiency as an excuse to lay off or refuse to hire women and sought to put a moratorium on the demand for creation of more jobs for women (Evenson 1986b:314).

The FMC leadership strongly criticized the subordination of women's equality to productivity and efficiency. Consequently, the Council of State was persuaded to pass Resolution 51 in 1980, setting aside almost five hundred thousand jobs for which women were to be given preferential consideration. Candidates considered for these positions require the consent of local workers' councils and are monitored by a special commission staffed by CTC and FMC representatives (Evenson 1986b:316). The FMC has also pressed for the equalization of pay for women entering nontraditional occupations such as law and medicine and has coordinated studies to assess the impact on women's rights of laws regulating occupational health and safety in an attempt to rescind paternalistic and overprotective legislation (Evenson 1986b:317, 322). This policy, however, has not been very effective in avoiding the assignment of work according to a "sexual division of labor" (Benglesdorf 1988b:126). This is consistent with Vilma Espín's insistence that women's rights are predicated on a "feminine, not feminist" conception of equality (Azicri 1979b:31). Accordingly, women fill jobs that are consistent with preconceptions about their temperament, ability, and interests and that carry the least risk of harm to their reproductive capacity (Benglesdorf 1988b:128).

Women now constitute 38.7 percent of the work force. Approximately 56 percent of middle- and upper-level technicians are women, including nearly 67 percent of all graduates in medical sciences (Espín 1991:50, 58). The FMC is attempting to increase the percentage of women holding leadership positions in the party (in 1990, 13 percent of the members of the Central Committee and 13.6 percent of the Politburo were women), in people's assemblies (in 1990, 17.1 percent of municipal delegates and 33.9 percent of National Assembly delegates were women), in ministries (in 1987, 25.4 percent of managers were women), and in mass organizations (in 1990, 22 percent of CTC leaders and 38.5 percent of Union of Young Communists [UJC] leaders were women) (Espín 1991).

Momentum was building in 1979 for even more extensive reforms in labor-management relations when the National Assembly appointed a special commission to investigate management abuses of workers' rights. Apparently, the commission had surveyed nearly 26 percent of work centers when the study was stopped. Although the final report was never completed, according to Fuller (1992:179), many of its findings were discussed in *Trabajadores*, the official publication of the CTC. Nevertheless, new labor legislation passed the following year constituted a significant setback in workers' rights. Decree Law 32 (1980) transferred jurisdiction over all disciplinary infractions to management while allowing the CTC to retain authority over cases involving workers' rights. In addition, a special appellate structure was abolished, rerouting all appeals through the regular courts. Penalties against management infractions also were stiffened in new Decree Law 36 (1982), but enforcement has been uneven.

Fuller (1992:201) reports extensive dissatisfaction with Decree Law 32 among the rank and file. Workers complained of management overzealousness in disciplining and dismissing workers who warranted less severe treatment. CTC surveys conducted in 1981 and 1983–84 indicated that Decree Law 32 was used twenty-five times more often than Decree Law 36 and that 1 out of every 6 workers was disciplined compared to 1 out of every 111 managers (Fuller 1992:202). The onset of the special period in 1990 seems to have revived support for consolidating the dispute resolution process into a single decisionmaking structure. Villa Clara province was chosen as the experimental site to implement what is called a "new experience" in dispute resolution (FBIS 1990c). Under this scheme, labor councils consist of one appointed representative each from management and the union and three elected worker representatives.

This body has jurisdiction over all disciplinary infractions and worker rights cases involving transfers or dismissals. Cases resulting in minor sanctions are final. However, appellate relief can be sought through the regular courts in cases involving temporary or permanent changes in a worker's employment status (FBIS 1990c). Such procedures are essential in that the number of workers expected to be displaced is conservatively estimated to be more than sixty thousand (FBIS 1991f).

State arbitration is one of the mechanisms for management accountability that ministry and planning officials have used until recently to review and control contractual relationships between enterprises. The State Arbitration System (OAE) was instituted by the Council of State in 1978 to assist the SDPE in securing proper resource utilization by enterprises. The OAE is responsible for regulating contractual relations between enterprises and suppliers, adjudicating disputes, conducting research, and advising ministry officials about problems that affect national economic objectives (Evenson 1986a:377). State arbitration in socialist states poses a particularly onerous threat to managers because they can be put in a double bind for exercising independent initiative. For example, contractual disputes frequently result from material shortages beyond any firm's direct control. Managers cope with shortage-induced contractual delays by arranging informal, unapproved agreements with suppliers to handle shortfalls. These same informal connections are exploited by unscrupulous managers to conduct various illicit transactions. Consequently, arbitration for contractual lapses makes the enterprise not only financially liable for nonperformance or negligence but also potentially subject to penal sanction for economic crimes. In these circumstances, enterprise legal advisers in socialist states must bend the law to conceal illegal arrangements from authorities that may or may not be indispensable to fulfillment of annual plans (Shelley 1984: 143–45).

During the first six years of its existence, the OAE caseload grew dramatically from 539 cases in 1981 to 14,000 in 1983 (Evenson 1986a: 381). Because the OAE was unable to handle this burgeoning load, jurisdiction, except for cases of national significance, was transferred in 1984 to provincial bodies (Evenson 1986a:381). Fuller (1992:280) reports that in 1988, 41,000 cases were under review by the national and provincial arbitration units. The OAE retained its advisory role to the Council of State and generally showed a greater facility in addressing national economic issues through research rather than through litigation. In 1991 the OAE's status as an independent agency was abolished. OAE staff members were reassigned to the State Committee for Labor and Social Security, where they continue to conduct economic research (FBIS 1991f:6).

Microbrigades and the Dilemma over Rights

Another innovation affecting union influence with uncertain implications for workers' rights has been the formation of work brigades. The idea of a microbrigade (mobile work units consisting of thirty individuals) was first proposed by Castro in 1970 as a method by which workers could qualify for and acquire housing (Mathéy 1989:69). Workers were released from their permanent employer and paid their normal salary. The model proved feasible, and by 1978 nearly eighty-two thousand homes had been constructed by thirty thousand brigade members. An acute housing shortage during the 1970s contributed to the popularity of microbrigades, as did the formula for allocation based on merit (i.e., good job performance and conduct) rather than need (Hamberg 1990:240).

Despite apparent popularity, the microbrigades were discontinued from 1978 to 1986 and were replaced by state construction brigades. The microbrigades appear to have been discontinued largely for political reasons (Hamberg 1990:246–47; Mathéy 1989:70; Mesa-Lago 1989:116). For example, the SDPE criticized the absence of cost-accounting controls and called into question the presumed inefficiency of using unskilled labor. Some observers questioned the validity of this concern because housing stock was considerably expanded at a cost ratio superior to that attained by state construction brigades (Zimbalist and Eckstein 1987:12; Hamberg 1986:600; 1990:247). The timing of the phaseout of microbrigades was significant since it coincided with the surge in export of construction workers and supplies abroad. This caused a scarcity of building materials for domestic housing, leading to a moratorium on housing construction in 1980 (Eckstein 1988:175).

Political factors appeared more salient than economics in explaining the demise and eventual resurgence of microbrigades. For example, management's contention that work-center productivity was adversely affected by the temporary loss of workers was belied by extensive overstaffing in state enterprises (Eckstein 1990:79). Management naturally resisted anything, such as policies designed to limit hoarding of labor and supplies, that would interfere with its ability to maximize its state budget allocation. Skilled construction workers, alienated by the higher wages paid to their unskilled counterparts, questioned the equity of this approach (Mathéy 1989:70). Finally, the most telling criticism of the microbrigade approach was that it excluded the people in greatest need for housing, such as unskilled workers, unemployed youth, and the elderly.

None of these political and technical concerns about microbrigades proved to be insurmountable, however, when Castro decided to reintroduce them on a broader scale in 1986. For example, management qualms about the depletion of the work force were placated by reimbursing enterprises for the loss of workers, a tactic whose economic logic is questionable. Castro mystified many Cuban scholars when he launched a policy of rectification in 1986, reversing the trend toward economic liberalization and decentralization and beckoning the restoration of *conciencia* and the primacy or moral incentives. Castro resurrected the image of Che Guevara in an appeal to the people for support by saying:

> Che was radically opposed to using and developing capitalist economic laws and categories in building socialism. . . . At a given moment some of Che's ideas were incorrectly interpreted and applied. Certainly no serious attempt was ever made to put them into practice and there came a time when ideas dramatically opposed to Che's economic thought began to take over. . . . Many of Che's ideas are relevant today. (Granma Weekly Review 1987:4)

To be certain, the deteriorating international economic climate and declining Cuban exports deepened Cuba's debt, contributing to a desperate demand for hard currency (Eckstein 1990:74; Zimbalist and Eckstein 1987:15–16). Cuba was also experiencing a substantial and growing state budget deficit that required the imposition of austerity measures. These serious economic difficulties (subsequently compounded by the precipitous withdrawal of Soviet aid) have contributed to some disagreement among Cuban observers as to how to interpret the purposes and foresee the consequences of rectification. For example, Mesa-Lago (1989:104) contends that the elimination of market mechanisms was motivated by flawed ideological reasons and will ultimately worsen the situation in Cuba. Eckstein (1990:68, 71) counters this view by arguing that the ideological rhetoric is misleading because the real aim of rectification is to eliminate bureaucratic abuses and corruption rather than combating the sins of market mechanisms. She concludes that this strategy has been ineffective, adding that "the Cuban government seemed to put much less emphasis on the values that Che stood for than it did when launching the RP [rectification policy] in 1986" (Eckstein 1990:79). However, if rectification is intended to stem the tide of bureaucratic corruption, it is difficult to understand how this could be accomplished without also eliminating the networks of private exchange underpining it.

I contend that the policies guiding rectification, as well as actions undertaken more recently during the special period, exhibit an ideological continuity with Guevara's conception of *lucha* and *conciencia* articulated in the 1960s. Guevara's vision of socialist persons was predicated on a complete reconstruction of every facet of capitalist labor, which included the culture of consumption, technologies of alienation, the selfish motivation for work, and inequalities based upon wealth, intelligence, and skill. The thread of continuity between the 1960s and 1990s can be discerned most clearly by examining precisely how brigades and contingents contribute to the fulfillment of Guevara's agenda for social reconstruction.

Eckstein (1990:79) persuasively describes how the microbrigade simultaneously addressed a number of interrelated bureaucratic problems associated with lowering the costs of production. Microbrigades could divert surplus labor to complete unfinished projects, thus avoiding layoffs; utilize materials more efficiently; and expand housing stock without adversely impacting investment in other sectors. This form of labor also provided greater flexibility in the assignment of tasks and length of working hours, regardless of job description or prescribed work norms (Mathey 1989:77). Beyond these economic benefits, however, the microbrigade offered an alternative way to overcome the most pervasive obstacles to the legitimacy of socialist development: alienation, absenteeism, demoralization, and diversion of effort into networks of exchange and consumption.

Microbrigades *pura* (brigades composed of work-center or enterprise employees) attempt to reduce alienation and demoralization in several ways. Members collectively develop a plan, assign tasks among themselves, and distribute wages according to individual output (Codina Jiménez 1987:135). Interestingly, the composition of the brigade takes into consideration similarity of interests and psychological compatibility to ensure harmonious integration (Codina Jiménez 1987:136). This may account for why participants reported higher morale, cooperativeness, and sense of collective responsibility than in regular work centers (Fuller 1992:282). However, brigade autonomy is also constrained. For example, reports vary as to whether leaders are elected by members or appointed by administrators (Codina Jiménez 1987:136; Fuller 1992:277). Work plans must be consistent with SDPE policies and regulations promulgated by the National Housing Institute (Hamberg 1986). Selection criteria for brigade membership are unclear, although work conduct and party ties are probably significant considerations.

In addition, brigade members do not determine the types of projects to which they are assigned, nor do they have any choice in the design or the construction materials used. They are rewarded, however, for innovative methods that involve the more efficient use of labor or materials. Also, brigade members must be willing to work longer hours and complete projects within a set time period. Only one-half of the completed dwellings are allocated to members. The other one-half are given to the local OPP for distribution among needy local residents or for schools, clinics, and day-care centers (Mathéy 1989:72).

The brigade concept was extended in 1987 to use unemployed or delinquent youth in neighborhood renovation programs. These microbrigades *sociales* helped remodel or enlarge existing stock while providing a guaranteed income and skills training to youth. An incidental effect of these brigades is that they supplant the burgeoning private market in residential remodeling, trading, and resale of homes and apartments (Hamberg 1986:608–9).

Perhaps the most ambitious and comprehensive example of how disciplinary techniques of social control are being used to increase productivity by countering absenteeism resulting from the search for scarce goods is the creation of the Blas Roca construction contingents. First begun in 1987, sixty Blas Roca contingents now have more than thirty-five thousand members. These contingents have been designed to determine if social and psychological principles can be applied to increase labor productivity. Cuban psychologists have developed a significant body of knowledge about the dynamics of personality development that can be incorporated into the design and testing of the contingent concept. (See Chapters 4 and 6.) For example, experimental studies of factors shaping moral development in small groups have demonstrated the importance of a strong role model, peer pressure, and a goal-oriented, task-driven environment for cultivating good work habits and positive attitudes. Psychologists have also determined that a worker's sense of dignity is governed, in part, by the value accorded specific tasks by the group and that the capacity to undertake extraordinary work assignments depends on whether they reinforce a sense of self-worth and self-esteem.

The contingents are organized to apply these and other principles of personality development. For example, contingent brigades are led by vanguard construction workers who provide training and supervise the work of inexperienced youth. Discipline is administered collectively through peer review, obviating reliance on prescribed labor codes and grievance procedures. Castro extolled the virtues of the Blas Roca contingents in commemoration of its third anniversary, underscoring the advantages of internal discipline and control:

> The Blas Roca demonstrated the importance of discipline and how discipline based on dignity, morality and men's pride, the collective spirit of men. . . . It completely distanced itself from the paternalistic, wordy, and we could even say, over-regulated norms of labor discipline in our country. . . . It was the collective workers that interpreted and applied discipline with a morality, an authority that even made the ones being disciplined admit to the fairness of their decisions. . . . It helped the youths a lot too. (FBIS 1990e:1)

The contingents are organized into mobile brigades and assigned to high-priority construction or agricultural projects that must be completed rapidly and efficiently. Consequently, contingent members are housed temporarily at the work site, with all essential needs provided for by the state. A physician and other staff are assigned to assure that members receive proper nutrition and rest in order to cope successfully with work-related stress or tension from long working hours. Castro boasted that the contingents had succeeded in disciplining and governing themselves by moral incentives alone because they were able, he said, "to create a family feeling throughout the worker's collective" (FBIS 1990e:2). Castro also asserted with an ironic paternalism that the contingents demonstrated "the importance of attention to the condition of the worker's material life, their comfort, food, and rest" (FBIS 1990e:2). The secret to their productivity, Castro reasoned, was "to give the worker whatever we can give him under the circumstances, to make him feel like his health is being cared for, to make him feel that his health is improving even though he works a lot. I think the Blas Roca has demonstrated, among other things, that work does not affect health" (FBIS 1990e:2).

Several of the resolutions on economic development adopted by the Fourth Party Congress in 1991 addressed the problem of labor discipline and the need to create a "climate of order and discipline" (Reed 1992:137–38). Resolution 13, for example, recommended adoption of more flexible forms of work organization and management. The contingents, among other experiments, were specifically singled out as exemplifying the "new and positive work concepts" needed to overcome barriers to increased economic growth. Castro made no secret of the fact that he opposed what he perceived to be a formalistic and legalistic approach to workers' rights. Instead, he has urged the adoption of more flexible work structures capable of adapting to new and uncertain contingencies facing Cuba in the special period. This poses a difficult dilemma for Cuban workers who have acquired greater job security by obtaining recognition for their rights.

Part 2

The Transition to New Strategies: Institutionalization and Regulation

4

The Family, Child Development, and Delinquency

By the end of the 1960s it had become evident that strategies of mobilization and redistribution were taking a toll on Cuban society. Crime and delinquency were on the rise, calling attention to the weaknesses of the popular courts and the organizational disarray of the judicial system. As a result of these trends and in light of a faltering economy, a national forum on internal order was convened in 1969. Experts were brought together to discuss possibilities for resolving the problems of declining productivity, delinquency, and disorder.

The national forum was significant for three reasons. First, it constituted the first systematic effort by Cuban leaders and jurists to determine how socialist legality could be translated into a constitutional regime governed by codes of criminal law and procedure. This led to the creation of a judicial commission, headed by Blas Roca Calderío, to draft a new constitution that included permanent institutions of representation and governance (this document was eventually ratified in 1976). Second, the Cuban leadership acknowledged the significant role the natural and social sciences could play in resolving institutional problems and overcoming barriers to Cuban social development. And, third, child development and community psychology (discussed in Chapter 6) emerged as dominant fields of applied knowledge. Professionals in these disciplines generated preventive techniques that promised to increase the capacity of medicine to promote societal well-being.

In a noteworthy speech on "self-criticism" presented to the FMC in 1970, enumerating the many mistakes committed during the 1960s, Castro announced that "subjective" conditions would form the new point of departure in revolutionary reconstruction:

> We repeat, the revolution is now entering a new phase; a much more serious, much more profound phase; one in which our resources of experience are greater than ever before; one in which the revolution will have to tackle

ever more complex problems with new methods, with the experiences accumulated through these years in the field where we can bring about a change in conditions—that is, in the subjective factor, in the human factor. . . . There are some objective factors that can and should be changed, but only man can effect such changes; only man can alter such conditions— which is why our effort can and should be directed toward man. (1983c :111)

In this chapter I examine why Cuban leaders reversed policies that deemphasized the family in socialism, explain why child growth and the conditions affecting moral development in group processes have become a preeminent object of research, and describe how the norms of revolutionary conduct are embodied in law and applied to handle the problems of delinquency, dissidence, and corruption.

The Dissolution and Renewal of the Family

The resolutions adopted by the forum in 1969 signaled a significant reversal of the radical policies pursued in the early years of the revolution. Guevara and other leaders actively sought to replace the family as the primary agent of socialization. This responsibility would be assumed by day-care centers, schools, and mass organizations. In fact, parents were expected to devote more time to voluntary activities that contributed to socialist development rather than to individualistic endeavors rooted in the nuclear family.

Three related factors appear salient to understanding why the regime found it necessary by the early 1970s to strengthen, rather than replace, the role of the family in a socialist state. First, the Family Code (1975) constituted an acknowledgment of women's increased participation in the work force (a little more than one-third of workers are women) by creating equal rights and responsibilities between husband and wife, including the care of children and home. Second, however, the demands on parents to participate in voluntary work with mass organizations and party-sponsored activities contributed to longer and more frequent absences from the home. Families became unstable, and children were not receiving adequate care or supervision. Increases in divorce and delinquency were two of the most important consequences. Consequently, parental responsibility for child-rearing was spelled out in great detail in these new laws. Third, Cuban psychologists and pediatricians convinced party officials of the importance of child development and the need for intervention and control of all factors bearing on well-being throughout the life cycle (García-Averasturi 1988:185–86). After conducting an initially successful campaign to reduce infant mortality, the regime experienced a sharp reversal in 1969, when infant deaths attributed to respiratory and intestinal diseases increased from 39 to 47.7 per 1,000 live births. This factor brought about a significant expansion of pre- and post-natal health services that dramatically increased the scope and frequency of intervention (Riveron et al. 1976:19–20).

The Family Code and the Code on Children and Youth (1978) are the most definitive expressions of the significance of child development to Cuban policymakers. Many provisions of these lengthy laws reflect professional judgments as to factors considered conducive to individual growth and development, family stability, and socialist development. Both laws were drafted by the juridicial committee of the Communist Party and circulated widely for input by mass organizations and citizens. The Women's Federation under Vilma Espín's leadership played a particularly active role in mobilizing its members to disseminate information about these laws through special assemblies around the country (Azicri 1979b:45–47).

Among other things, the Family Code was designed to correct many of the inequities and abuses associated with the prerevolutionary relationship between husband and wife. It accomplishes this through a variety of provisions regulating marriage, divorce, and the equal sharing of child-rearing responsibilities and housework. In addition, it is intended to prescribe in explicit terms the kinds of roles it expects parents to assume in a socialist society. Parental responsibilities are stipulated in some detail:

> Keeping the children under their guardianship and care; making every possible effort to provide them with a stable home and adequate nourishment; caring for their health and personal hygiene; providing them with the means of recreation fitting their age which are within their possibilities; giving them proper protection; seeing to their good behavior; and cooperating with authorities in trying to overcome any situation or environmental factor that may have an unfavorable effect on their training and development. (Family Code 1980:229)

Parents are also expected to fulfill the needs of the country by "seeing to the education of their children; inculcating them with love for learning; seeing to it that they attend school; seeing to their adequate technical, scientific, and cultural improvement in keeping with their aptitudes and vocations and the demands posed by the country's development; and collaborating with the educational authorities in school programs and activities" (Family Code 1980:230).

The Code on Children and Youth specifically identifies programs and special projects coordinated by these groups and prescribes in some detail eligibility, target populations, activities, and other rules bearing on participation. There is also a rather extensive elaboration of the kinds of health-related requirements that pregnant mothers must observe before and after childbirth as well as the forms of discipline and supervision appropriate for child-rearing (Finlay 1981).

Espín (1991:66–68) acknowledged in an interview in 1989 that, despite the gains Cuban women had attained in the workplace, full equality had yet to be achieved in the family. Survey research revealed that traditional attitudes about the division of labor in the home prevailed. Male and female respondents alike believed that it was "proper" for women to manage the home, even though this meant the assumption of a "double role" for mothers who worked, and that men were "naturally" more equipped to assume leadership roles outside the family (Espín 1991:71). Working mothers also continued to bear primary responsibility for child-rearing. Espín expressed concern about the "serious distortions" in personality development likely to occur when fathers remained uninvolved in the upbringing of their children (Espín 1991:71).

Espín (1991:75) indicated that insufficient attention had been paid to the role of women and needs of families and that a special family study group had been established in 1989 to study both issues. Participants in the study group were drawn from several organizations, which included the UJC's Center for Social Studies, the National Sex Education Group, the Commission for Social Attention and Prevention, the Academy of Sciences, the Ministry of Justice, and psychologists from the University of Havana and the Ministry of Education. The study group will attempt to consolidate the findings of past social research as well as conduct new studies. Espín (1991:76) indicated that the family study group will combine efforts, exchange knowledge, debate approaches and research designs, and "establish guidelines, and needs by identifying women's position in the different stages of our development."

Cuban policymakers' dual attempt to promote egalitarian changes in traditional sex roles that strengthen, rather than weaken, family structures sharply contrasts with how Chinese leaders are handling this issue. When Deng Xiaoping introduced his program for political and economic modernization in 1976, the family was viewed primarily as a site to effectuate a dramatic reduction in population growth and facilitate urbanization and industrialization. Consequently, the "one child per couple" policy, initiated in 1980, has been used largely as an instrument of social control rather than reform. For example, the state has asserted control over many functions traditionally assumed by the extended family, such as who, when, and how a person may marry and the number of children that can be conceived, by delegating these powers to work centers (Grant 1989:25; Troyer 1989:31–32). Moreover, the erosion of family structure and the increased emphasis on individualism have contributed to higher rates of urban delinquency in China than were experienced in the past (Rojek 1989:90–96).

Intrusive techniques to bring down the rate of population growth in rural China have fared little better. Yang (1989:32–35) contends, for example, that techniques for classifying, rewarding, and/or penalizing women according to the prescribed norms of reproduction have simply substituted a grid of social disciplines for the traditional mechanisms of social hierarchy and conformity based on class and status. The use of financial incentives (and penalties) and land grants have increased opportunities for corruption while reinforcing traditional sex roles in the family (White 1987:291, 307). Brigade members responsible for implementing one-child policies have found numerous ways to grant exceptions, and peasants remain unconvinced that smaller households produce larger incomes. Moreover, rural wage policies discriminate against women, who receive only 70 to 80 percent of what their male counterparts earn.

Child Growth, Learning, and Moral Development Under Socialism

A significant impetus to research in child development occurred in 1971 when the Children's Institute was established, under the direction of Vilma Espín, to coordinate childhood education and welfare. Its mission is very similar to that of the U.S. Children's Bureau established in 1912—to integrate and coordinate all children's institutions, to train staff, and to sponsor research by professionals in medicine, psychology, and the social sciences (Cravens 1985). One of its first initiatives (like that of the Children's Bureau) was to conduct a longitudinal study that would yield national norms of growth and development. This study, other research, and experimental programs were instrumental in bringing about major changes in health care policy and approaches to child development as well as in stimulating professionalization of juvenile justice (Wald 1978:128).

The National Growth Study conducted from 1972 to 1973 was carried out in collaboration with two British experts, one of whom, Dr. J.M. Tanner, is a proponent of a "catch-up" theory of growth (Jordan et al. 1975). Developing countries such as Cuba were attempting to overcome nutritional deficits and other environmental factors contributing to a high infant mortality rate or otherwise inhibiting normal patterns of biological growth. A study of this kind would provide baseline data about growth rates among children from different age groups and geographic areas with which to measure the effectiveness of health policies and other interventions. One of the study coordinators interviewed by

Wald (1978:111) indicated that the intent was to derive norms or indicators of "well-being" that reflected "our own cultural and physiological reality." The Cuban growth study is frequently cited in the literature as a textbook example of the use of random sampling from a well-defined population to yield an accurate forecast of long-term changes in the growth and health profile of the whole population (Eveleth 1986:230; Goldstein 1986:64). Follow-up studies indicated measurable improvements in growth rates, as specified by the ratio between height and weight and as indicated by the earlier maturation of Cuban girls compared to their European counterparts (Jordan 1979; Eveleth 1986:230).

The catch-up hypothesis advanced by Tanner would have been especially appealing to Cuban leaders such as Che Guevara because he was strongly interested in identifying all factors, including biomedical ones, that might accelerate the creation of a new socialist person. Guevara (1968b:131) likened underdevelopment to a "teratological" (i.e., growth deformity) phenomenon. Dependency stunted and deformed individuals, preventing them from attaining a natural, well-proportioned physical stature and coordinated behavior. Tanner's (1963; 1986) theory, first explicated before conducting the Cuban study, provided an explanation for why growth processes resume at an accelerated rate (and, conversely, "catch down," or decelerate, after temporary spurts) after being retarded by some intervening factor. Tanner argues that human growth is governed by a target-seeking mechanism regulated chemically by the brain. Consequently, the velocity of growth will be automatically adjusted (assuming the deprivation is brief) to compensate for periods of growth that either undershoot or overshoot the normal proportionate relationship among height, weight, and size of body parts. Cuban scientists have continued to conduct laboratory studies of growth mechanisms. Also, since the early 1980s Castro has dedicated enormous resources to biomedical research in order to identify and control the neurochemical agents believed to regulate the processes of biological growth (see Chapter 7).

Systematic experimental research on child development was slow to develop in Cuba, primarily because of a shortage of trained psychologists (Bernal 1985). Psychology was not recognized as an independent field of inquiry until the late 1960s. The first distinguished graduates of the University of Havana, such as Fernando González Rey in child development and Lourdes García-Averasturi in community health psychology, received extensive academic training in the Soviet Union. Consequently, Cuban psychologists have been influenced strongly by Soviet theorists and experimentalists such as Lev Vygotsky, Aleksei Leontiev, and their followers, who include Boris Lomov, Piotr Gal'perin, Daniel Elkonin, and Maia Lisina.

These psychologists have advanced the "activity" theory of child development (Kozulin 1986), whose basic assumption is that human thought and personality are a product of social activities undertaken to reconstruct and control the environment. They argue against the theory popularized by Jean Piaget that mature cognitive and moral development occurs only after the passage from an ego-centered stage of nonrational thought to more socially complex situations requiring logical thought and rule-governed behavior (Elkonin, Zaporozhets, and Zinchenko 1971; Valsiner 1988:126–27). Instead, they contend that the logical form of reasoning is not as important in development as is the nature of the activity used to engage the child in the transition from pre-verbal to verbal reasoning processes (Valsiner 1988:214–15). Children effectively communicate and "interact" with adults throughout development largely because they share the same medium (i.e., objects and tasks) through which their activity occurs. Therefore, the primary objective of child development consists of helping the child acquire the technical capabilities to solve increasingly more complex problems in ways that contribute to the welfare of the group and society as a whole.

The influence of Soviet thinking on Cuban developmental psychology can best be grasped by understanding the meaning of and relationship among four key concepts: activity, attitude, communication, and inter-action. The term *activity* is not used by Soviet psychologists to refer to a stimulus-response conception of behavior. Instead, an activity, as Leontiev defines it, involves goal-directed behavior in which a method of operation is selected to complete a task and thus achieve a goal. Children attempt to devise a solution to a problem (e.g., determining the character-istics and potential uses of objects) through what is termed *orienting-exploratory behavior* (Elkonin, Zaporozhets, and Zinchenko 1971). Activity involves physical experimentation and symbol formation whereby a child gradually accumulates sufficient experience to master tasks through a process of logical reasoning. Adults can play a decisive role in the learning process by directing the child toward the adoption of opti-mum methods and strategies for problem solving.

The meaning that Soviet and Cuban psychologists assign to the terms *attitude* and *motivation* also are contrary to those understood by North American psychologists. These differences are not idiosyncratic or cul-tural but are derived from the findings of experimental studies. American psychologists, for example, define an attitude as a disposition to react either positively or negatively to ideas (Fishbein 1967:8). Motives are usu-ally understood to constitute reasons or intentions for doing something. Attitudes can influence motives by inducing feelings sufficient to prompt behavior. Soviet experimentalists in child development such as Lisina argue that motives are not a product of internal psychological states but rather emerge from a dynamic relationship forged between child and adult to cooperatively define and achieve some common objective. The Soviet conception of attitude also differs in an important sense from its North American counterpart. An attitude entails, not an implicit disposition for or against an idea, but a readiness to react and respond to a situation in the most socially effective way possible, no matter how attractive or undesirable the conditions may be.

Not surprisingly, Soviet psychologists such as Lisina and Elkonin have gravitated toward experimental study of how social interaction contributes to child development. They consider interactions between children and adults to constitute a special kind of communication involving the goal of mutual understanding (Valsiner 1988:244–45). For example, Elkonin (1971:178) has determined that the infant's struggle to master language is facilitated by being challenged by adults to correctly match the sound of words with the appropriate behavior they imply. Adults help children grasp the meaning of words by enabling them to experience how the words are embodied in concrete activity.

Lisina contends that social interaction not only satisfies children's need for attention and emotional reinforcement but also demonstrates how cooperation is instrumental to the attainment of individual ends. Interaction with adults stimulates the learning process, enabling children to express their needs with greater precision through increased cognitive control of the operations involved in problem solving. Lisina argues that the reciprocal bond formed between knowledge and affection through interactive learning provides a motive for mutual cooperation and understanding. Children learn that the effectiveness of joint activity is governed not only by the adequacy with which they appraise their own needs and capacities but also by the accuracy with which they comprehend and anticipate the needs and expectations of others.

González Rey has become the foremost Cuban exponent of the conceptions of child development advanced by Lisina and Elkonin. González Rey (1987:58) describes how the Soviet conceptions of attitude and motivation are systematically interrelated in action: "An attitude provides the form in which motives are structured in concrete manifestations of personality regarding objects, situations and other people through an integrated system of expression, which includes all components of a system of valuation and emotional expression."

González Rey believes that studies of attitude formation and the role of communication in moral development will yield norms with which to regulate and control the social processes involved in the construction of a socialist society. But such a goal cannot be attained, González Rey (1987:51) concedes, until Cuban psychologists obtain more detailed knowledge about the conditions in which deficits in affective or cognitive dimensions of development are likely to occur, particularly during childhood and adolescence.

González Rey's endorsement of this line of inquiry should be tempered by a frank recognition of two of the more conspicuous weaknesses of "activity" psychology. First, it may be highly misleading to draw inferences about norms of individual development based on relationships between child and adult because there is not only a fundamental difference in cognitive capacity but also an inequality of power. The presumption that the adult can best determine the most appropriate methods and techniques by which the child achieves his or her aims is an unwarranted justification of paternalism. Research in the United States on motor development (Thelen 1990; Thelen and Ulrich 1991), for example, demonstrates that the child's freedom to select and control the strategy and techniques used in problem solving is intrinsic to the learning process. Moreover, McGraw (1943), a pioneering growth scientist, found that progressive development is more likely to occur when learning encourages anticipation and judgment without prior intervention (Bergenn et al. 1992).

Second, even though effective communication requires some degree of shared meanings, this does not mean that we must impute some special ontological status to objects or techniques beyond their various uses or exchange value. Nor is mutual understanding impossible in the absence of a consensus on the ethics and norms of human conduct. Collective action occurs under conditions of uncertainty, and methods are often employed that involve unknown risks and unforeseeable consequences for the participants. Moreover, those participating in criminal enterprises and networks in socialist states justify their activities by arguing that the social benefits of their services outweigh the costs and that self-interest provides a better motive for cooperation than do altruism and social commitment.

Group Associations and Individual Conduct

Nevertheless, Cuban psychologists believe that the causes of many developmental disorders resulting in crime and delinquency can be traced to deficiencies in group structures or processes. This holistic point of view is derived from the belief that collective activity is mediated by the goals and tasks chosen by the group. Consequently, individuals engaged in joint activities acquire new characteristics that cannot be defined by, or reduced to, idiosyncratic traits or roles assumed by any single member of the group. Group member behavior is unified through shared perceptions and mutual understandings that enable coordinated and integrated responses to situations insoluble by individual intervention. According to Soviet psychologist Artur Petrovski, "diffuse groups" (e.g., illicit networks) fail to reach the threshold of integrated action because the social significance (i.e., likelihood of contributing to social equity and progress) of the goals and tasks is ill-defined, minimizing the motivation for selflessness and cooperation (Valsiner 1988:276). Members of groups not governed by joint activity and possessing asocial or antisocial values will tend, according to Petrovski, to exhibit an aimlessness and a cynicism and to be incapable of anything more than episodic, self-serving, and transient relationships with each other.

Cuban psychologists seem to have avoided some of the more obvious logical difficulties entailed in using Petrovski's method of differentiating personality traits solely according to characteristics of the groups to which they belong. For example, Fuentes Avila (1982) contends that group cohesiveness by itself does not account for the effectiveness of group performance. Highly developed groups are characterized by their capacity to translate members' values into concrete attitudes supportive of a specific activity that promotes the welfare of the group as a whole. Significantly, the fact that sympathetic relationships are formed only among members of developed groups seems to account for their success, compared to undeveloped groups, in cooperating in an activity involving a common objective (Fuentes Avila 1982:123–24). In this regard, adolescents involved in social and legal transgressions have been found to lack a well-developed conception of moral behavior and therefore are unable to critically assess the appropriateness or judge the seriousness of associating with those involved in criminal conduct (Roca Perara et al. 1982). Thus, criminal conduct is more likely to be sanctioned when group members operate in microenvironments isolated from the influence of those governed by a more rigorous sense of self-discipline and social obligation (Vasallo Barrueta 1986).

Delinquency and the Second Economy

As previously noted, the National Forum on Internal Order called attention to the need to deal more effectively with a rising crime rate. By the late 1960s, a substantial percentage of serious crimes were being committed by youth. In 1967, for example, minors committed 41 percent of all property crimes; in 1968 they accounted for 27 percent of thefts and 23 percent of all violent robberies. Truancy had risen to large proportions by 1969, with more than four hundred thousand students neither attending school nor working. Nearly one-half of all truants in 1972 were sixteen years old—a prime age for delinquency.

Cuban jurists and criminologists dominated the discourse on crime and delinquency until the mid-1970s. They advanced a variety of explanations for delinquency that deflected criticism from the potential weaknesses and adverse consequences of the legal strategies for social development undertaken in the previous decade. These theories generally reflected the thinking of Soviet criminologists, who sought explanations of deviance and crime that did not implicate or condemn institutions operating according to socialist principles (Connor 1971:107–9). During this time Soviet criminologists ignored psychological research on child development and instead propounded theories about the bourgeois origin of crime (Connor 1971:176–85).

The belief persists among Cuban jurists that socialist legality will eventually eradicate pernicious bourgeois values undermining family stability. For example, a former president of the Cuban Supreme Court contends that an analysis of adolescents who commit crimes would reveal that they "are influenced by a series of factors inherited from the old society and how these factors are transmitted from fathers to their children, and of course we shall have for a long time these persons influenced by the past" (Hernández de Aramas 1977:301–2). Or, as a Cuban law professor observes, the bourgeois family is an instrument of private property, relegating love and sexual relations to a secondary role. He contends, according to Azicri (1985:324), that only socialist legality can abolish the exploitative motives that inhibit the formation of family relationships predicated on trust and affection.

Castro seems to have been divided on the causes of delinquency. Until the late 1960s, he subscribed to the view that delinquency was due to vestiges of capitalist consciousness transmitted through prerevolutionary parents to offspring, including negative influences from the United States such as the "hippie" culture. During these years Castro was confident that Cubans in general would acquire the discipline required to resist capitalist influences and behavior and would readily accept sacrifices when they underwent experiences similar to those the guerrillas faced during the insurrection. Special work units were created in the military for delinquent youth, and work camps were established, such as the one at the Isle of Pines (now Isle of Youth), in the mid-1960s in order to remove youth from bad family environments and expose them to the conditions of sacrifice and discipline in which a revolutionary consciousness could be formed.

By the late 1960s, however, Castro was being confronted with mounting evidence that parents who were conscientious revolutionaries were unknowingly contributing to delinquency by committing errors in child-rearing and discipline that contributed to pathological reactions (Isaiev 1967; Torroella 1966; 1968). Castro began to cite these factors in speeches and interviews (Salas 1979b:24–28). Nevertheless, Castro (1976:53–54) continued to express uncertainty as to an appropriate response because of an essential ambiguity in the motives of delinquent offenders: "There comes a time when it is almost impossible to distinguish between the counterrevolutionary delinquent and the common criminal, because many of the individuals who committed counterrevolutionary acts in the past are now committing these common crimes." Thus, Castro's support for a preventive, rather than a punitive, strategy toward delinquency was contingent upon its demonstrable effectiveness in intervening and controlling the sites (i.e., family, school, and work) at which attitudes are formed and motives adopted to generate behavior consistent with the norms of socialist development.

In the intervening years, studies and experimental intervention programs conducted by psychologists and other professionals have led Castro to express a stronger interest in and support of research on the causes of delinquency. For example, in a speech before the Fourth Congress of the FMC in March 1985, Castro commented extensively on the findings of sixteen interdisciplinary longitudinal studies of children from families with problem or delinquent behavior commissioned by the Ministry of the Interior. Castro's reference to these studies is remarkable as it represents the first time that he publicly acknowledged the value of such behavioral studies and linked them to specific policies:

> I have here some data or research by different agencies. It is interesting to see why we have children with anti-social behavior, why we have children with criminal tendencies and how the family has a bearing on the academic standing of children. . . . As we can see, the nature of the family has a direct bearing on the moral upbringing of minors. In the case of children with negative behavior, relatives do not have a correct educational policy, which is manifested in the lack of positive role models, lack of supervision in the fulfillment of work norms and the use of disciplinary methods based on physical punishment. There is a lack of affection in these relationships leading to a break in adequate communication with adults or other members of the family. This in turn means that minors do not develop positive personality traits since they lack adequate means to assimilate socially accepted norms and values.
>
> I think these studies are very interesting and they should be continued and intensified if we want to discover the concrete and precise causes of these problems. . . .
>
> You can have perfect schools and teachers, but if the child starts skipping school and then doesn't do his homework, nobody controls him and he roams the streets until late at night, the schools are of little value. We can use scientific data to precisely determine the influence of these factors on the upbringing of children and youth. (Granma Weekly Review 1985:5, 7)

Castro urged additional follow-up studies, for example, to determine the causes of a rising divorce rate and suggested a comparative study of why the incidence of urban delinquency was so much larger than in rural areas (Granma Weekly Review 1985:7). Castro's reaction is certainly indicative of an increased receptiveness to the use of psychological and epidemiological studies in policymaking—that is, as long as they do not contradict his belief that parents of delinquent youth show poor revolutionary integration. Psychiatric epidemiological studies have not demonstrated thus far that nonparticipation is necessarily associated with nonintegration or mental illness. Nevertheless, studies conducted by the Psychiatric Institute of Havana conclude that nonintegrated individuals exhibit, according to Camayd-Freixas (1985a:165), a "statistically greater incidence of involutional neurosis than the socially integrated."

As noted earlier, research on delinquency and education is of particular interest to Castro because of his belief that absenteeism from school (and work), poor academic performance, and crime are directly related, a position he has maintained since the late 1960s. Truancy from school and absenteeism from youth groups and other party-sponsored activities have increased sharply. In 1972 approximately 215,500 students between the ages of six and sixteen were neither in school nor working (Salas 1979b:20). More recently, it was estimated that as many as 250,000 youth twelve to sixteen years old were neither working nor studying. Also, poor school performance is viewed as a contrivance to escape work obligations that carry dubious distinctions, such as nomination to positions that sometimes entail service in internationalist missions. The Ministry of Education reported in 1986 that 75 percent of 96,000 middle-level secondary school students had failed semester exams (Baloyra 1987:11). Significantly, 68 percent had flunked the first makeup exam, and 59 percent had still failed the final makeup. Among the students interviewed in a recent study, 58 percent admitted to not working as hard as they could (Baloyra 1987:12). Poor school performance appears related to dissatisfaction with the quality of teaching and perceived uninterest in student performance.

Not surprisingly, research has been conducted to determine why so many students perform poorly in school or repeat grades so frequently. Control group studies in 1974 found, for example, that repeaters were more likely to have parents with low IQs (intelligence quotients) and/or who suffered from psychological problems. Also, delinquents were more likely to have a lower IQ and exhibit psychotic traits when compared with normal children. More recently, Castro discussed the results of a longitudinal control group study that examined family-related factors that might account for absenteeism. Negative aspects of family life that contributed to absenteeism and poor school performance included a high divorce rate; lax, inconsistent, or inappropriate discipline, such as corporal punishment; a large family; a record of unemployment and criminal involvement by parents; a lack of emotional care; and a lack of participation in mass organizations (Granma Weekly Review 1985:7). These study findings are interesting in their rather strong emphasis on the character and behavioral defects of parents—a view taking on renewed vigor in the United States—and the conspicuous exclusion of peer group influence as a contributing factor.

Fidel Castro has not only shown an increased receptivity to psychological explanations of crime and delinquency grounded in theories of childhood and personality but has also encouraged a revival of Freudian theories. Significantly, Freudian doctrines have experienced a resurgence after a long period of censure in the early years of the revolution. For example, in June 1990 Cuban psychologists sponsored the third Latin American meeting on "Marxist Psychology and Psychoanalysis." Participants were invited to exchange experiences with therapeutic procedures, professional training, clinical practice, and experimental studies (Granma Weekly Review 1985:4).

Perhaps the most significant element of the Code on Children and Youth is the administrative provision regarding delinquency. The code establishes a process by which professional judgments are blended into the methods for the adjudication of delinquent youth. A municipal evaluation committee, consisting of a psychologist, psychiatrist, teacher, doctor, lawyer, and social worker, assists the court having jurisdiction (there are no special juvenile courts in Cuba) by conducting a diagnostic examination that includes medical and psychological tests and then recommending a disposition.

In 1982 two significant changes were made in juvenile justice policy (Baloyra 1987:19). First, Law Decree 64 decriminalized many crimes committed by youth, increasing the age from twelve to sixteen for youth subject to prosecution as adults. Second, the administration of juvenile corrections was removed from the National Revolutionary Police and placed under the Directorate of Minors, a new division created within the Ministry of the Interior. The directorate shares administrative control over Councils for the Assistance of Minors with the National Revolutionary Police, the former assuming diagnostic responsibilities once performed by the Municipal Evaluation Committees. The new law also specified and enlarged the treatment modalities available to handle juvenile offenders (Shaw 1982:25–26). This clearly signaled a shift toward less restrictive alternatives, enabling professionals to assume greater responsibility and control (Lerman 1982). These changes reflected the increased influence of professionals and national officials over juvenile justice and the weakening of local community and provincial standards governing judicial response.

In addition to these adjudicatory and treatment processes, in 1978 the Commission for Social Prevention was established within the Communist Party's municipal committees. The commission comprises representatives of the FMC, CDRs, CTC, Ministry of Education, Ministry of Justice, Ministry of Public Health, and Young Communist League (YCL). Members of this commission provide assistance to families, neighbors, friends, teachers, and students in resolving or correcting patterns of minor antisocial behavior. If commission members are unable to correct a situation, they prepare a report for the Councils for Assistance to Minors recommending some other course of action (Baloyra 1987:21). These profiles, introduced in 1974, include academic data, biological facts (presumably height, weight, and any medical problems), socioeconomic data, personality traits, and character evaluations regarding revolutionary integration. The files are revised on a yearly basis and follow the student throughout school and become a part of a "work dossier" compiled during adult life (Finlay 1981:260; Wald 1978:293).

The National Revolutionary Police has reassumed some overlapping administrative control of the activities of the Commission for Social Prevention through the sector chief assigned to each neighborhood (Baloyra 1987:21). In addition, the Front for Vigilance and Public Order and the Front for Education and Prevention, both presumably composed of trusted party cadres, have been assigned to oversee neighborhood prevention activities by CDRs and other groups. The emergence of this supervisory (and apparently parallel) layer of administrative party control is consistent with the increased role that the national government has assumed in delinquency prevention policy. But it also suggests that government officials have been clearly dissatisfied with the results of previous efforts by local officials and laypersons. Officials are now determined to obtain a sharper distinction between serious and minor offenders and between political and nonpolitical forms of delinquency than has been provided thus far.

The relationship between delinquency and the dramatic growth of an underground economy is being taken very seriously by the Cuban Academy of Sciences, which is sponsoring an interdisciplinary, multiyear study of this criminal phenomenon. Dr. Fernando Barral, a psychiatrist, criminologist, and research associate working on the project, attributes the cause of a youth-dominated underground economy to what he calls "the mercantilization of criminality" (Grogg 1991:30). Barral explains that this new crime phenomenon is threatening to socialist regimes because its structure conceals the true dimensions of its impact on socialist distribution, making it indistinguishable from legitimate economic enterprises. One reason for this situation is the covert collaboration between persons in legitimate occupations with access to goods and marginal criminals, who act as intermediaries for potential buyers desiring to purchase these goods. Another reason is that these transactions generate huge amounts of capital whose source is difficult to trace. These funds can be reinvested in state-regulated enterprises or used to purchase hard currency, subsequently recirculated in the regular economy, or to initiate a new series of unregulated transactions.

Barral contends that this "mercantile stratum" first appeared when the SDPE was implemented in the mid-1970s (Grogg 1991:31). The evidence he provides to support this contention is that the SDPE introduced the criterion of profitability and a blind or unconscious trust in market forces. Although acknowledging that scarcity plays an important role in the proportions of the black market, Barral argues that the greatest threat is psychological and attitudinal. As more people are implicated in this illegal economy, Barral warns, a "mercantilist mentality" spreads contagiously, infecting people with complacency and tolerance and thus hastening the advent of ideological transformation, such as that occurring in Eastern Europe. Barral explains the demise of socialism there by reasoning that "when the latent pressure to conform with socialism disappeared as a result of *perestroika* and its consequences, that capitalist ideology suddenly was left unconcealed and in a dominant position" (Grogg 1991:32). Although Barral's theory may exaggerate the significance of subjective attitudes, his thesis correctly reveals how much regime legitimacy depends on the perception that only those who consistently make a productive contribution to society and do so according to the rules can expect to be rewarded and advanced in their chosen occupation.

Dissidence and Corruption

It is difficult to accurately gauge the scope of political dissidence in Cuba for essentially two reasons. First, the U.S. government has actively exploited political dissension in Cuba in an international campaign (involving the participation of exiled anti-Castro groups) to condemn and discredit the Cuban government for the abuse of human rights. For example, the Reagan administration orchestrated unsuccessful campaigns in 1986, 1987, and 1988 to persuade the U.N. General Assembly and the U.N. Human Rights Commission to condemn and sanction Cuba for various alleged abuses that included harassment, torture, and imprisonment of rights activists (Platt 1988:41–43). These accusations prompted a number of rights organizations, such as Amnesty International (1987), the New York City Bar Association (Henkin et al. 1988), and Americas Watch (1984), to send delegations to Cuba to investigate the treatment of political dissidents. Even though many of the most serious charges were determined to be unfounded or exaggerated, delegations concurred that dissident groups were unable to freely criticize government policies without the fear and threat of retaliation.

An accurate estimate of the true dimensions and political significance of dissident activity in Cuba is also hampered by the tendency of the Cuban leadership to dismiss some forms of dissent as oppositional and counterrevolutionary. Castro and other officials exercise enormous discretion to decide the boundary between criticism reflecting honest differences and attacks on the legitimacy of the regime (Rabkin 1987). The ambiguity inherent in this distinction worked to Castro's advantage when he attacked the credibility of Ricardo Bofill Pages, founder of the first human rights commission in Cuba in the early 1980s. Castro questioned Bofill's motives by contending that he had been imprisoned in 1967 for associating with the Escalante microfaction and that he was merely seeking political asylum in order to collaborate with Cuban exiles (García-Crews 1988:236).

However, Cuban officials have encountered more difficulty suppressing the activities of a successor to Bofill's group formed by Elizardo Sánchez Santa Cruz (a former professor at Havana University) in 1987 and called the Cuban Commission for Human Rights and National Reconciliation (CCHRNC). Sánchez has chosen, unlike his predecessor, to gain legal recognition of the CCHRNC by working privately within the system, bringing rights abuses to the attention of authorities. Even though Cuban authorities have arrested Sánchez several times, he has firmly rejected political asylum and continues to attract attention to the issue of rights in Cuba.

In 1989 Sánchez and Sebastian Arcos Bergnes, vice president of the Cuban Human Rights Committee, accused the Cuban government of using electric shock treatments and psychoactive drugs to punish political dissidents (Schanche 1989). This was the first time that such abuses, which had become commonplace in the Soviet Union, were reported in Cuba. Although the charges have never been independently verified by the United Nations or other international rights groups, such as Amnesty International, an incident at the Psychiatric Hospital in Havana lends some credence to these allegations. In June 1991 two distinguished neuroscientists were convicted of planning to blow up the Neurology and Neurosurgery Institute in Havana during a visit by Castro in 1990. In addition, two other doctors at the institute were charged with disseminating "enemy propaganda" in relation to the incident (FBIS 1991g). However, it is not known what motivated the assassination attempt and subsequent protests.

As other dissident groups surface, the government has used more overt tactics to discredit those who are arrested by getting them to publicly repudiate their claim to legitimacy. For example, in one alleged incident members of a clandestine branch of the Pro–Human Rights Youth Association were arrested for plotting acts of sabotage and were interviewed about the charges on television. Interestingly, one collaborator, who held the post of municipal delegate in a district in Havana, declared that he had worked as a liaison among the youth association, other disaffected informal groups, and several foreign embassies, including the U.S. Interests Section (FBIS 1990a:11). If reports such as this are not contrived, then it would appear that network linkages forged between groups with different interests are undergoing some degree of politicization. These groups pose a serious threat to the regime because they could join in a conspiracy in which unheard criticisms circulate and gain the momentum to erupt in unanticipated forms of resistance.

The scandal involving General Arnaldo Ochoa and officials of the Ministry of the Interior in 1989 presented perhaps the most serious challenge to the legitimacy of the Cuban leadership since the Escalante affair. General Ochoa, a highly respected officer and commander of Cuban forces in Angola, was accused of insubordination and participation in black market activities in Angola and was implicated circumstantially in drug dealing with the Medellín cartel in Colombia. Ochoa and three others were tried in a highly publicized trial and executed. Shortly thereafter, Minister of the Interior José Abrantes and a half-dozen subordinates were arrested and given stiff prison terms for corruption; scores of additional resignations were tendered from ministry staff (Rabkin 1991:185). Castro denied any political undertones to the scandal. Nevertheless, General Rafael del Pino (1987:55–57), who defected from Cuba in 1987, claimed nearly a year before the incident that Cuban counterintelligence had discovered a high degree of discontent among officers and that he expected a crackdown.

A number of clues were provided by both Fidel and Raúl Castro that General Ochoa's popularity was perceived as a threat to the regime (Habel 1991; Preston 1989). For example, Ochoa angered Raúl Castro because he may have taken sides with Soviet advisers in disregarding some of the latter's instructions in conducting military operations in Angola. Raúl Castro expressed a strong personal animosity toward Ochoa, replacing him with his own protégés. He also hinted that Ochoa may have favored Soviet policies of *glasnost* by inviting any officers who might favor this approach to go to Hungary or Poland, where such reforms had led to the restoration of market economies (Preston 1989:26).

Interestingly, Raúl Castro also condemned Ochoa for his temerity in questioning the value of Fidel Castro's health-care programs (Preston 1989:26). In this regard, it is important to remember that the military has on a number of occasions (mostly during the 1960s) organized and conducted voluntary work programs, including special training and prevention programs for delinquents. No doubt many officers who are experienced guerrillas believe that they possess valuable expertise in addressing problems of social development and quite possibly feel arbitrarily excluded from involvement in this realm. Although Ochoa and others never denied their participation in illegal exchange activities, an extensive network involving the military and the Ministry of the Interior that took exception to Castro's investment and policy priorities in social development had surfaced.

5

The Structure of Policymaking, Influence, and Accountability

Recent observers of Cuban political and economic development disagree regarding the extent to which the Cuban revolution has been institutionalized (Azicri 1979a). Some argue that if institutionalization includes economic and political independence, a process of leadership succession, and a civilian-controlled government administration (Horowitz 1979:84–89), then the Cuban revolution has not been institutionalized. Cuba is now suffering a perilous economic crisis precipitated by the collapse of trade with Eastern Europe and withdrawal of Soviet financial, technical, and political support; no process of succession exists; and this special period in peacetime has resulted in Castro's increased concentration of power. Others point out that participation in substantive policymaking remains limited in Cuba (González 1979:81) and that the military and Communist Party continue to exercise monopolistic power (Vellinga 1976:263–68). Moreover, the incredible delay of sixteen years before a constitution was adopted creates skepticism about the seriousness with which the Communist Party takes its principles, institutional structures, and rights. Nevertheless, it is also clear that Cuba has established a permanent framework of political authority and participation able to sustain social order through law and governance and involving some degree of decentralization of control. This achievement has led observers such as Azicri (1979a; 1988), Casal (1975), and Benglesdorf (1990) to argue that mechanisms such as legislative assemblies and party congresses that facilitate and transmit criticism of leadership, and thus promote accountability and change, are in place.

In this chapter, I contend that a more promising way to approach this contentious issue of governance is to focus on the actual processes, rather than on the formal structures, through which policies are formulated and implemented. The literature on policy analysis is replete with examples of the importance of studying how policy is implemented before drawing inferences about the structure of power in centralized and decentralized political systems (see, for example, Hjern and Hull 1982; Sabatier 1986). Consequently, I describe the sequence of phases through which a policy passes as it is translated into concrete programs and identify those stages in which specific institutional structures contribute to (or impede) meeting policy goals and objectives. In addition, I examine how the party's role has evolved since the 1960s and assess what the changing composition of the PCC Central Committee and Politburo implies about the relative influence that old cadres and professionals exert in policymaking and implementation processes. Finally, I evaluate recent criticisms of the weaknesses of local and national assemblies and their delegates within the perspective of the larger structural constraints that limit representation and inhibit accountability.

Policy Development and Implementation Processes

From the outset, Castro was confronted with uncertainty and great political risks in attempting to alter the sequence and accelerate the processes of socialist development. Consequently, he adopted a pragmatic approach to problem solving that capitalized on his charismatic leadership and capacity to arouse spontaneous action without forfeiting his need to form judgments based on the best available experimental evidence (Fagen 1965). Castro perceptively understood that opposition to social reconstruction could not be overcome simply by a peremptory exercise of power. Instead, he has skillfully developed and institutionalized a strategic policymaking process reflecting his distinctive personality traits and leadership style to ensure broad input and feedback without diminishing his or the party's authority and leverage over national policy. This process enables the Cuban leadership to integrate information derived from participation and resistance into a cycle through which knowledge is continually transformed into new modes of participation and techniques of social organization and control.

The sequence of policy formation and implementation consists of several discernible phases, including issue resolution, experimentation, evaluation, dissemination, implementation, and adjustment. First, issues surface and are resolved when there is mounting evidence corroborated through different channels, such as heads of mass organizations, party officials serving on the Politburo, or ministry officials reporting to the Council of State, that an ongoing policy is failing or is unlikely to achieve its objectives. The Politburo, or Political Bureau, is the highest decision-making body of the Cuban Communist Party. It consists of 25 members (including Castro) elected by the 225 members of the Central Committee of the PCC. Party congresses can serve as an important sounding board for problems and potential solutions, although Castro usually determines the agenda and priorities for action. The Escalante microfaction, the 1970 sugar harvest debacle, and the policy of rectification begun in 1986 are three of the more spectacular examples of how extensive opposition, resistance, and/or evasion provoked major changes in policy direction. Castro now deploys a small personal staff and party operatives to continually monitor and make incremental adjustments, when necessary, to avert such situations. Castro relies heavily on information generated by his "coordination and support team," which handles troubleshooting assignments around the country. Two of his staff (a chemist and a physician) possess additional authority through their positions on the Politburo, while two others serve as alternate members (Reed 1992:168–69).

Castro also generates information by using interdisciplinary study groups or commissions to help formulate and implement policy responses to problems. For example, Blas Roca Calderío, a former Politburo member who died in 1987, served Castro well in coordinating a task force to draft a constitution, and Vilma Espín, head of the FMC, helped overcome resistance to women's equality by conducting an effective educational campaign to increase awareness of and support for the Family Code in 1976. Castro's reliance on coordination in problemsolving and policy implementation provides flexibility in the concentration of personnel and resources while limiting dependency on ministry officials and the chain of command.

By the time the stage of experimentation begins, Castro and other leaders are usually committed to seeing a program implemented as a national policy. This is not to say that input at this stage is trivial. To the contrary, the experimental phase provides an opportunity to evaluate concrete experiences, thus enabling correction of unforeseen difficulties before replication nationwide. The significance of the experimental phase was well illustrated when Castro introduced the OPP on an experimental basis in 1974:

> When I say "experiment," I don't mean that we're experimenting with whether or not to have People's Power or that our party isn't definitely planning to apply the idea throughout the country. It is an experiment only in the sense that we're testing the methods, mechanisms, regulations, and everything else related to the establishment of People's Power before these things are put into effect on a nationwide scale. In other words, the experiment will help us perfect the idea—but the idea is to apply these principles throughout the country. (1983f:194)

Two weaknesses that undermined the experiment in popular justice and People's Courts were the absence of effective coordination with the existing judiciary and the lack of systematic evaluation. Both deficiencies were corrected in the Matanzas experiment in local representation. This experiment involved the attempt to comprehensively integrate and devolve administration and control over the delivery of health, education, housing, and other services to the local level. In addition, a team of social scientists, including psychologists from the National Group of Psychology and the Ministry of Public Health, were chosen to evaluate the effectiveness of increased coordination between municipal governance and community health prevention (García-Averasturi 1985:121; Camayd-Freixas and Uriate 1980; Pérez-Stable 1985:133–34). This analysis helped sort out problems involving overlapping ministry jurisdictions and demonstrated to Castro (1983f; 201–3) the feasibility of expanding local responsibility and accountability without diminishing national authority and control.

Since then, psychologists and other social scientists have been given broad responsibility to evaluate and advise policymakers about ongoing and experimental programs in health, education, labor, and other areas (García-Averasturi 1988). Castro frequently participates in extended evaluation processes, questioning and conversing with professionals involved in experimental programs in order to increase his ability to appraise strengths and weaknesses.

The next phase of the policy process involves the broad dissemination of the results of the experimental stage to increase public awareness; generate criticism, debate, and support; and ensure that those who assume supervisory or professional roles as either party leaders, bureaucrats, or professionals are adequately prepared to fulfill their new responsibilities. Solicitation of formal approval by the Council of State and the National Assembly lends legitimacy to subsequent implementation. The Council of State (headed by Castro) is generally vested with the authority to implement (or annul) resolutions passed by the National Assembly and to oversee state administrative activities.

Castro makes effective use of appearences before the National Assembly to project to Cuban citizens an extremely compelling image of how he expects a policy or program to work. For example, Castro used a striking military metaphor to describe the preventive mission that the new family doctors (discussed in Chapter 7) would perform by calling them "sentries for health." The detailed knowledge accumulated from the experimental phase, including quantitative performance projections, is deployed by Castro with great dexterity; he disarms critics with his mastery of enormous detail while dispelling misconceptions and rumors associated with any major change in the status quo. Mass organizations provide an important conduit through which Castro's message can be transmitted, reacted to, and approved by the people; and he frequently assigns one to assume a lead role in implementing the policy. The CDRs and the FMC also help widely circulate and obtain feedback on proposed laws, including the constitution approved in 1976, which was estimated to have been read in draft form by more than 3 million Cubans.

Complex policies are usually implemented in stages so that regulations and resources can be adjusted to reflect ongoing progress and unanticipated needs. For example, the implementation of the family doctor program has been limited largely to Havana and other cities because of a shortage of buildings for office space and insufficient medical graduates specially trained in "integrated medicine" to fill rural posts. In addition, time is required to properly integrate a new program into the existing administrative apparatus and governance structures. Problems of coordination have to be worked out between existing service providers, such as polyclinics and general hospitals; overlapping roles of mass organizations, such as the FMC and the YCL, must be sorted out and clarified; and professional conflicts have to be resolved.

During this critical period, resistance or intransigence becomes a significant factor shaping outcomes. In essence, large-scale programs such as the family doctor, which involves the erection of a new network superimposed on existing ones, pose a host of unforeseen challenges that can be worked out only through experience. That is why Castro aptly characterized the family doctor program as a "breeding ground for new ideas, a laboratory for new ideas" (FBIS, 1991a:8). Implementation marks only one phase of a knowledge cycle whereby reaction to policies stimulates development of new techniques of control, which are subsequently inserted into the ongoing policy cycle.

The boundary between formal governance processes and the domain of administrative regulation and informal social control in Cuba is uncertain largely because social policies undergo a continual series of adjustments after implementation commences. Changes introduced into ongoing programs sometimes reflect Castro's disenchantment with or alarm at the uncontrolled growth of party functionaries or intermediate bureaucracies of mass organizations such as the CDRs. Castro has usually handled excessive bureaucracy by tactical reorganizations that result in substantial staff reductions and/or by superimposition or layering in new programs, such as the People's Councils, accountable directly to him. Moreover, since the inception of the OPP, a series of laws have been passed renationalizing control over many of the services initially entrusted to local government.

It also is noteworthy that since 1979, decree laws issued by the Council of State have been considered equivalent in constitutional and judicial standing to laws passed by the National Assembly (Azicri 1988). Since that time, decree laws have been used with increased frequency, as previously described, to establish uniform national policy on controversial issues (e.g., delinquency or housing) where consensus is unlikely and professional expertise is brought to bear. Although some of these changes reflect an interest in achieving greater equity and consistency in the administration of these policies, they also involve the contraction of citizen control and the expansion of professional expertise in policy processes.

The Changing Role and Influence of Cadres and Professionals in Cuban Politics

Old party cadres (i.e., guerrillas or bureaucratic functionaries who have acquired positions of leadership through sacrifice and loyalty) and professionals (specialists with advanced degrees in law, economics, medicine, psychology, or other fields who have acquired prestige and influence through expertise) play pivotal, although sometimes conflicting, roles in the implementation of social policy in Cuba (Fitzgerald 1990b). The role party cadres play in policy processes has evolved from direct involvement in administration to more indirect and flexible forms of influence and intervention. Domínguez (1989a:56) argues that the PCC has not adapted very well to the conflicting pressures involved in assuming a less active leadership role. In the early years of the revolution, party members played a vanguard resolver role, exercising authority to intercede and correct problems as they saw fit. For reasons already discussed, this resulted in an appalling degree of corruption and indifference. The OPP was designed to rectify the abuse of power by removing the party from administration and limiting its role to that of *atender*, providing guidance and supervision to induce appropriate conduct. As Raúl Castro (1983:234) insists, "The party does not administer; . . . it must never meddle in the daily routine work of the organs of People's Power."

Despite this new role definition, party cadres were faced with the dilemma of reconciling their constitutional task of *controlar* in the active sense of exercising leadership and guidance with a more passive sense of overseeing at a distance. Domínguez (1989a:57) suggests that Castro now has become disenchanted with passive control because it only reinforced reliance on material incentives and the primacy of informal networks of power and privilege. Subsequent purges in 1987 led to the discipline or removal of thousands of party members who had overstepped the boundaries of legality, affecting nearly one-quarter of the total membership (Domínguez 1989a:58–59).

In 1990 additional sweeping changes in party structure and role were undertaken (subsequently approved at the Fourth Party Congress in October 1991) that virtually eliminated intermediate administrative bureaus. The functional departments of the Central Committee Secretariat were consolidated from nineteen to nine, and staff was reduced by 50 percent. Significantly, a new party role was enunciated akin to that performed by the *guerrilla foco* more than three decades earlier. The party leadership was urged to adopt the "broadest possible methods and work styles, thereby eliminating *frentismo* (factionalism) and *homologuismo* (exclusivity) (Granma Weekly Review 1990c:9). The "basic tenet" of the party was to "fulfill its role of orientation and control with an increasingly all encompassing and multilateral vision, adapting its organization in a flexible manner to the characteristics of the territory in which it is operating and the specific priorities of the task at hand" (Granma Weekly Review 1990C:9). By this reckoning, party members may intervene in administrative matters if such action is deemed necessary to correct the situation.

Professionals have not experienced the same type or severity of role conflict and change as party cadres have, but their increased participation in the evaluation and implementation of policy has placed them in a very sensitive position with respect to accountability for policy success and failure. They must operate in a system of "dual subordination" that makes them responsible simultaneously to local leaders and ministry officials, thus increasing the potential for divided loyalty. Kenworthy (1985:197) observes that this system gives a significant advantage to policymakers because it provides "a way to bring to the surface the politics inherent in policy implementation, so that lower and middle level bureaucrats and their *socias* (cronies) do not subvert policy goals set on high." In this regard, the Cuban leadership has explicitly stated that it expects professionals to devote and confine their attention to the evaluation and improvement of the implementation of its policies. In a speech to economists in 1977, former SDPE director Humberto Pérez was most emphatic about their role in economic planning:

> Of course, this work of yours should take place with full freedom. . . . About questions of principle, of course, about an elemental question of revolutionary discipline, neither seminars should be held or investigations made, but about questions of how to implement these principles, a form of aid to their better implementation is precisely that you examine without limitations of any type the implementation already made, even when these have the character of law, or a decree, of a resolution of a ministry, or a promulgation of any type. (Fitzgerald 1990a:195)

Although professionals are clearly not intended to make policy, they sometimes are held responsible for policy failures. For example, Castro blamed the deficiencies of the SDPE on Humberto Pérez, claiming he followed the advice of the shortsighted technocrats. Castro also contended that hospital-based medical specialists were responsible for undermining the performance of polyclinics. Despite these criticisms, professionals are important intermediaries in policymaking processes who can, if they choose, cooperate with or resist the Cuban leadership in policy implementation processes. Contrary to Rabkin's (1988:37) assertion, technocrats and professionals have not become "politically marginalized" in Cuba (as I illustrate in subsequent chapters); they have assumed significant advisory roles in the experimental and implementation phases of the policymaking process.

One important indicator of the relative influence that professionals have acquired compared to that of other institutional elites (i.e., military officers, ministry officials, and general secretaries of mass organizations) is reflected in their increased membership on the Central Committee and the Politburo. LeoGrande (1978:23) was one of the first Cuban observers to spot incipient signs of a shift away from "revolutionary" and toward "managerial modernizers." Significantly, he found no persuasive evidence that this shift signaled a change in the balance of power between the so called *fidelista* and *raulista* groups, but he suggested instead the existence of multiple factions with crosscutting institutional ties. The proportion of military compared to other institutional representatives in party leadership positions remained relatively stable (although declining in absolute terms) through the Fourth Party Congress in 1991. Moreover, the Ochoa scandal (discussed in Chapter 4) showed that the military does not constitute a unified or monolithic interest group but rather consists of potential critics of regime policies likely to seek collaborative ties with like-minded leaders of civilian institutions, such as the Ministry of the Interior.

The trend toward professionalization of the Central Committee grew more distinct in the Third and Fourth Party Congresses in 1986 and 1991. For example, Domínguez (1988:7) found that whereas nearly 75 percent of party members had a ninth grade education or more in 1986, 78 percent of Central Committee members appointed during the Third Party Congress had a university education. Domínguez (1988:6) observes that this pattern of "overrepresentation" of the university educated reversed the "underrepresentation" characterstic of party leadership fifteen years earlier. This "reversal of democratization," as Domínguez (1988:7) calls it, installed personnel "more capable of governing but also less representative."

The number of university graduates appointed to the Central Committee increased another 11 percent during the Fourth Party Congress held in October 1991. In addition, more members came from the sciences; they now occupied 14.2 percent of the 225 positions. The most conspicuous changes in the composition of the Politburo were due to the replacement of six revolutionary pioneers among the fourteen persons who became new members of the twenty-five-member body. Among those stepping down were Armando Hart, former minister of culture, and Roberto Viega, former general secretary of the CTC. Vilma Espín, who had been harshly criticized during the preCongress discussions for not effectively advancing women's rights (Reed 1992:156), lost her position on the Central Committee but retained the presidency of the FMC. Castro justified the large turnover of the Politburo on the grounds that the revolutionary leadership needed to be revitalized with new blood in order to ensure the continuity of the revolution in the years ahead (Reed 1992:158).

One of the more significant changes in managerial assignments of Politburo members occurred with the appointment of José Ramón Machado Ventura to head the new Department of Organization. This department, which was created one year before the Fourth Party Congress (Granma Weekly Review 1990c), consolidates administrative control over the previously separate departments of organization, general affairs, mass organizations, state and judicial organs, basic industry, and consumption and creates a new department for cadre policy. Machado Ventura, a physician and former minister of public health who played a seminal role in the reorganization of the health-care system begun in the mid-1970s, is likely to approach the integration of social and legal policies from a strategic medical or health perspective (as has been the case in the family doctor program discussed in Chapter 6). He also may seek increased professionalization of party cadres, including recruitment of more physicians and scientists.

Assessing the Effectiveness of the OPP

The OPP was created with four objectives in mind. First, a process was begun to determine what kinds of services could best be provided at national, provincial, and local levels of government. Second, faltering party leadership could be revived and strengthened (and perhaps shielded from direct accountability for failure) by narrowing its responsibility to policy prescription, thereby shedding an operational role. Third, local elections would enable citizens to hold administrators accountable for services through oversight; problems and difficulties experienced at this level could then advance to regional and national assemblies for resolution. Fourth, mass organizations would perform a new role as intermediaries between national and local officials. Instead of reliance on the diffuse tactics of mobilization, mass organizations could now develop more specialized and particularistic forms of activities directly linked to the provision of services.

Understood in these terms, the development of representative government in Cuba since 1974, when it was experimentally tested in Matanzas province, should not be condemned, as some authors have done, as superfluous and ceremonial or uncritically celebrated as a fundamental innovation in democratic decisionmaking. Instead, it should be viewed as a method of decentralizing decisionmaking in the delivery of local services. In some ways this development is similar to policies of inter-governmental federalism begun in the late 1960s in the United States to promote greater local control while increasing accountability to Congress and the executive establishment.

There is, however, growing evidence questioning whether the OPP promotes accountability and effectively represents the needs and in-terests of Cuban citizens. Criticisms converging from different sources challenge the viability of the constitutional principle of dual subor-dination as the centerpiece of democratic centralism because it is unable to sustain the distinction between governance by representation and administration.

Perhaps the strongest evidence of the depth of disenchantment with the OPP surprisingly came from a survey of 847 respondents, repre-senting a cross-section of different occupations and conducted by the Cuban journal *Bohemia* (Carrobello et al. 1990). Two of the most signifi-cant results of the survey indicated that nearly 50 percent of the respon-dents felt that OPP delegates "did not have sufficient authority to solve problems in [their] district" and that 40.9 percent did not have complete confidence in their delegate (Carrobello et al. 1990:6). In addition, 40 per-cent did not feel fully involved in governance, and 55.8 percent of the respondents thought that the current form of government needed im-provement. Overall, the vast majority of the respondents (70.5 percent) concurred with the statement that improvement could best be achieved by "seeking more flexible, efficient methods of government administra-tion without changing existing structures" (Carrobello et al. 1990:6).

Follow-up interviews conducted with some of the respondents uncov-ered three overriding criticisms. First, respondents noted that delegates suffered from both role confusion and role conflict. Delegates acted as though they were expected to solve problems administratively when, in fact, the constitution specifically limited them to representation. Many respondents attributed this problem to ambiguity in how they were sup-posed to relate to central state ministries. For example, one respondent blamed poor delegate role perceptions and deficient performance on the failure of the National Assembly to publish and disseminate studies that would increase knowledge and awareness of the relation between local problems and national policy.

Excessive bureaucracy was also singled out as contributing to weak-nesses in local representation. Respondents complained of unnecessary paperwork, complex procedures, and the labyrinthine hierarchy they had to surmount in order to obtain assistance. Respondents criticized meetings in which delegates "rendered accounts" as tedious, time consuming, and poorly attended by CDR representatives, who were usually incapable of helping rectify a situation. Citizens also complained of frustration with long delays after which they found out that the delegate could do nothing.

In a final concern reflecting the pervasiveness of informal networks, citizens protested rampant favoritism. Respondents stressed that the real problem was not the lack of resources, but their improper allocation. Significantly, citizens typically characterized their delegate's job as consisting primarily of "begging for favors" rather than transmitting the legitimate demands of constituents (Carrobello et al. 1990:6). The most telling evidence of corruption was the material advantages reaped by the delegate and his or her cronies (Carrobello et al. 1990:7).

The Chinese experienced many of these same difficulties when they undertook reforms in 1980 to provide for the direct election of delegates in county-level elections (McCormick 1987). Previously, elections had been held in factories and involved a slate of candidates all chosen by the local party leadership. The new system dropped the requirement that candidates be party members. Not surprisingly, local party cadres perceived these reforms as a threat to their authority, which was based upon a patron-client relationship. Consequently, party cadres vigorously resisted reform by using gerrymandering, influence peddling, and other tactics to weaken voter independence. They also attempted to bypass standing committees in an effort to divert ministry resources and staff to projects that served specific political interests. Therefore, delegates were pressured to confine their input to the particularistic concerns of their districts rather than to raise issues of national significance (McCormick 1987:407).

From another quarter, Juan Escalona, former justice minister and newly appointed president of the National Assembly, acknowledges in an interview in *Bohemia* (Tesoro 1990) the difficulties delegates are having in adopting a consistent role. However, contrary to the opinions of survey respondents, Escalona contends that governance and administration can be distinguished conceptually and that the delegates' role should and could be limited to the former. According to Escalona, governance involves "the analysis of the cause of problems," and " the setting priorities on the sequence in which problems need to be solved" (Tesoro 1990:50). Governance also includes "enforcement" to ensure that "laws are complied with in an equal way," Escalona stresses, "and not on the basis of the interpretation made of them in a given municipality (Tesoro 1990:50). In contrast, administration is understood by Escalona to consist of the execution of tasks requiring "immediate action" to solve daily problems.

Curiously, Escalona's solution to the problem of inadequate governance would further weaken, rather than strengthen, the role of the National Assembly in policymaking and governance. He proposes the creation of a new executive committee selected by himself that would function independently of the National Assembly. Escalona's rationale for this is that deputies serving on this committee could assume administrative duties on a full-time basis without risking a conflict of interest. This proposal, however, technically violates the constitutional principle of dual subordination by removing administrators from direct accountability to the National Assembly. Moreover, such a move does little to close the gap between the promise and the reality of representative government by providing a concrete delegate role in policymaking.

Castro's assessment of the problems of local governance in his 1990 address to the National Assembly led him to draw conclusions somewhat at odds with the primary concerns expressed by respondents in the *Bohemia* survey. Castro's complaint is twofold. First, he believes that local delegates have too much power and discretion. Castro argues that the goal of equity and uniformity has been subverted by the practice of allowing each municipality to choose its own methods of administration (FBIS 1990g:14). Second, he attributes weaknesses in delegate representation to the delegates' lack of accountability to central state administrators. The image Castro conjures in his description of the municipal governments as "bottomless lakes" is one of remoteness, indifference, and corruption (FBIS 1990b:14). Castro demands that localities be "penetrated" (a task now being undertaken by the People's Councils), recommending metaphorically that the National Assembly should "select a group of surgeons . . . to dissect the municipalities in order to determine who was in charge, what they were doing" (FBIS 1990b:13). Castro strongly supports Escalona's proposal, which he believes will correct these problems by increasing the level of professionalism.

These and other deficiencies of the OPP were discussed at the Fourth Party Congress. Party delegates resolved that participation could be substantially increased by providing for the direct election of delegates of both the provincial and national assemblies. They also recommended that studies be undertaken to find ways to strengthen delegates' "leadership and administration at the intermediary and grassroots level" by providing more preparation and training (Reed 1992:123). This was proposed so that delegates could become more knowledgeable about the relationship between local problems and national issues addressed in the planning process. Perhaps the most important resolutions pertained to the problematic relationship between delegates and state administrative agencies. Party members recommended that the roles of state agencies at the municipal and provincial levels be distinguished according to whether they performed representative (i.e., mass organizations) or executive-administrative functions (i.e., ministries providing health, education, or other services) and that their respective spheres of operation be directed by the presidents of the local and provincial assemblies. This proposal was intended to improve coordination between mass organizations and service providers and increase the participation of members of the UJC and other mass organizations in assembly discussions.

Despite these reforms, the commencement of a special period in peacetime in 1990 has further consolidated the control that Castro and the Politburo wield in governing Cuban society. Castro defined the special period to consist of contingency planning for the possible partial or complete loss of oil and supplies resulting from the discontinuation of trade with the Soviet Union and Eastern Europe. Such an eventuality, Castro declared, "would be equivalent to the situation we call a special period in time of war. . . . We must foresee the worst possible situation that would confront the country in a special period in peacetime and plan what to do" (Granma Weekly Review 1990a:4).

Castro contended that the special period justified two important extensions in his discretionary power. First, he declared henceforth that he would exercise exclusive authority and control over supplies (i.e., food, water, and oil) and industries of strategic importance to the country. Industries Castro considered strategically significant included pharmaceuticals, biotechnology, and tourism because they generated hard currency from abroad. Second, the Politburo was empowered to appoint additional members at any time without approval of the party congress (Reed 1992:157).

The potential that proposed changes in the OPP have in rejuvenating governance processes in Cuba is uncertain. An important measure of their effectiveness will turn upon whether delegates can acquire sufficient expertise and the independence necessary to overcome parochial and paternalistic party interests so that they can exercise stronger policymaking and oversight functions. The reforms undertaken by the Chinese in the National People's Congress are instructive in this regard. For example, in 1982 national deputies were given authority to conduct legislative forecasting and coordinate the lawmaking process. They performed this role skillfully by expanding access to policymaking, increasing bargaining, and standardizing the rule-making process (O'Brien 1990:163–64). Deputies also became more effective in gaining larger allocations to their particular districts in support of enterprise zones and other policy innovations that did not entail complete party consensus.

However, newly created standing committees rarely exercised independence and typically served, O'Brien 1990:164–71) notes, as proxies for the Communist Party by advancing criticism judiciously and constructively, with an eye out for resistance, evasion, and noncompliance.

Thus far, delegates to the Cuban National Assembly have been able only rarely to effectively link local problems, such as the lack of construction materials, with issues of national importance, such as housing policies (Ritter 1988; Benglesdorf 1990). This may increase their dependence upon professionals as intermediaries in the difficult and politically sensitive task of coordinating and overseeing the provision of health and other services. Nevertheless, rational and representative policies involving the just allocation of scarce resources can neither be held hostage by party cadres nor result in the peremptory imposition of professional judgment. The uncertainty lies in determining correctly how to navigate between or perhaps reconcile the demands of patronage-based exchange networks and knowledge-based service networks.

Part 3

The Professionalization
of Prevention

6

A Psychology for Well-Being

In an interview following his defection to the United States, General Rafael del Pino (1987:51) revealed that Castro relies heavily on work groups coordinated by his personal staff to identify and analyze key issues of major policy decisions. Interestingly, in characterizing their activities, General del Pino (1987:51) noted, "Within these groups there is a team of sociologists and psychologists who are constantly assessing and analyzing the internal situation of the country. As soon as there is a tad of dissatisfaction and discontent, this group immediately recommends that [Castro] 'open the safety valve.'"

This could easily be dismissed as a throwaway statement by a disaffected Cuban general. However, there is some validity in his assertion that psychologists, among other scientists, play an increasingly systematic, rather than an episodic, role in the formulation of policies for social development. Their primary contribution, however, does not consist of placating discontent but rather of enabling individuals to realize their full potential under socialism. Psychologists are attempting to identify the cognitive, attitudinal, and moral factors that lead individuals and groups to adopt positive values, to prefer cooperation and collaboration to individualism, and to be motivated to make a productive contribution to society.

In this chapter, I describe how psychologists have significantly influenced strategies for social development in Cuba. Several factors have considerably eased the stress of occupational transformation for Cuban psychologists in the transition to socialism compared to that experienced by other Cuban professionals as well as psychologists in other socialist states. The development of psychological theory has not been hampered by the rancor and divisiveness that beset Soviet and Chinese theorists as a result of recurrent political purges. Moreover, Cuban psychologists, unlike their counterparts in medicine, for example, were unconstrained by a previously defined organizational structure and institutional roles and thus could adopt structures and roles pertinent to the needs and goals of the revolutionary leadership. Cuban psychologists have also developed experimental studies and innovative diagnostic tests that have proved to be effective levers in the attempt to transform the curative orientation of medicine to a preventive one. Consequently, psychological theories and techniques are increasing the capacity of the Cuban leadership to integrate knowledge from diverse fields in order to mount a coordinated and comprehensive approach to human development and social planning.

Theoretical Psychology and Cuban Socialism

The development of the field of psychology under socialism has been particularly noteworthy, until recently, for its dismal record of failure. Psychologists have found it extremely difficult to explain individual behavior without risking criticism and scorn by colleagues and party officials for subverting the principles of Marxism-Leninism. Proponents of lines of psychological inquiry considered inconsistent with communist ideology were suppressed or driven underground during Stalin's purges in the 1930s and forbidden in China for over a decade as a result of Mao's Cultural Revolution begun in the mid-1960s.

For example, state institutional support was withdrawn from Soviet pioneering child psychologists such as Lev Vygotsky, whose work failed to reflect a Pavlovian orientation (Kozulin 1984:62–82). Nevertheless, his studies on language development did attract adherents in Moscow among members of the "Kharkov school," which included Aleksei Leontiev, Aleksandr Luria, Alexander Zaporozhets, Daniel Elkonin, and Lidia Bozhovich, whose ideas have been formative in the development of Cuban psychology. These investigators were able to advance Vygotsky's promising line of inquiry by officially denouncing his work and then cleverly distinguishing their premises from Vygotsky's (Kozulin 1984; Valsiner 1988:208–9). Vygotsky's theory that the child helps construct the environment in which she or he develops by independently assigning specific meanings to objects according to the use or need they satisfy was considered an ideological deviation (Valsiner 1988:114–49). The members of the Kharkov school were careful to stress that they were more interested in determining how children's activities were structured by adults and in demonstrating how meanings were evoked by strategies children learned from adults to manipulate objects in problem-solving situations (Valsiner 1988:209–10).

The Cultural Revolution in China also adversely affected research in developmental psychology. During the 1950s Chinese psychologists followed the work of Russian "reactologists," such as Konstantin Kornilov and Anatoly Smirnov, whose ideas were considered consistent with Maoist ideology. Kornilov believed that all human activity was a product of conditioning and that socialist consciousness consisted of the dialectical unity of contrasting physiological and ideological factors to form consistent patterns of behavior (Valsiner 1988:83–84). Smirnov held that memory played a significant role in the content and control of thought processes. Their ideas squared well with the importance Mao attached to thought control, which was epitomized by the required use of his "little red book" of sayings to guide the process of self-criticism.

By the late 1950s, however, Chinese psychologists had initiated experimental and field studies in child development. Factors accounting for differences in motivation and moral development were explored, as was an analysis of the influence of attitudes on learning processes and work (Chin and Chin 1969:165–77). The Cultural Revolution brought these studies to a halt in 1966. Communist officials denounced these analyses as bourgeois and castigated psychologists for suggesting that ideological indoctrination alone was incapable of converting the "mass line" into mass conformity (Livingston and Lowinger 1983:216–17). Consequently, all teaching and research in psychology were ended, major journals ceased publication, and scholars were cut off from the revolution in child development research occurring in the Soviet Union and the United States. Psychologists were unable to resume developmental studies until academic recognition was restored in 1978, and controversy still persists as to how to reconcile new trends in developmental psychology with regime ideology under Deng Xiaoping.

Cuban psychologists have been fortunate in avoiding the disruption and discord exemplified by the Soviet and Chinese experiences. They have been spared from the ideologically provoked conflict, recrimination, and discontinuity besetting psychology in those socialist states. Leading Cuban theorists and experimentalists farsightedly elected to build on a body of research in child development that, although controversial, showed promise in addressing issues of motivation and conscience pertinent to the construction of Cuban socialism. Moreover, Cuban psychologists have maintained a surprising degree of continuity with prerevolutionary precursors such as José Agustín Caballero (1762–1835), Felix Varona (1788–1853), and Enrique José Varona (1844–1933), each of whom saw the importance of activity, experience, and language in education and child development (Bernal 1985:223–25).

Professional articles in psychological theory, experimental research, and clinical practice are generally published in one of three main journals. The *Boletín de Psicología* (Bulletin of Psychology), first published in 1978, is devoted primarily but not exclusively to experimental and clinical studies. This journal includes reports of national and provincial research and conferences and covers several related topics of interest to both theorists and clinicians. For example, a substantial number of studies of infants, children, and adolescents in groups in a variety of different settings (i.e., schools, work centers, clinics) are published that examine factors affecting normal personality development. (See, for example, Fernández González 1987; Herrera Jiménez et al. 1987; Ojalvo Mitrani and Mijailovna Andreieva 1981; Pérez Rodríguez 1982; Pérez Lovelle 1985; Quintana Mendoza et al. 1984; Solé Arrondo 1987; Sosa Cardentey and Martínez Perigod 1984; Váldez Marín 1980; 1983.)

Cuban psychologists, unlike their North American counterparts, do not believe that emotional disorders can be explained solely by individual dysfunctions, nor do they attribute learning difficulties primarily to sensorimotor defects. Their experimental group research suggests, for example, that the level of frustration, embarrassment, and tension felt by individual members is governed by their perception of the fairness, consistency, and seriousness with which other members adhere to group rules and norms (de la Caridad Martín Martín et al. 1986; Riera Milián 1987). Psychologists also discovered that pathological anxiety and some types of neuroses can be better understood by examining how they are manifested or triggered in group situations (Herrera Jiménez, Díaz Castillo et al. 1987; Portero Cabrera 1984). In addition to these studies, Cuban psychologists have conducted comparative research to identify whether learning disabilities associated with mental retardation (Herrera Jiménez et al. 1987) and disordered reasoning processes characteristic of those suffering from chronic neuroses (Herrera Jiménez 1988) might be explained by some underlying variation in the sequence or pattern of cognitive processes.

Contributors to the *Boletín de Psicología* are also developing psychological techniques to influence individual behavior and group interaction. For example, instruments to measure suggestibility have been tested (Hernández Meléndez 1984), including the susceptibility to rumors (Román Hernández et al. 1985). There also is an interest in understanding how new groups are formed (Pérez Vera 1984), and how artificial intelligence can be applied in medicine and psychology (Ilizástigui Pérez and Ageenko 1986).

The *Revista Cubana de Psicología* (Journal of Cuban Psychology) was started in 1985 by the Society of Cuban Psychologists. This journal focuses primarily on theoretical and methodological issues involved in the study of personality development, including the assessment of the problems and issues involved in testing and clinical diagnosis. Articles deal with the full range of factors involved in personality development in play, school, and work such as motivations, attitudes, values, and beliefs. Yet, strangely, with the exception of one article (Bernal and Isern 1986) criticizing the ideology of family therapy, there is a conspicuous absence of any analysis of the role of the family in child development. This seems to run counter to recent policies acknowledging the importance of the family in Cuban society but probably reflects the belief that individual development can be more effectively influenced and changed through group processes than through family intervention. The work of Cuba's leading theorist, González Rey (1986; 1987), is featured prominently along with seminal articles exploring the significance of language, communication, attitudes, and values in cognitive development and moral self-regulation. Also, an interest is evidenced in assessing the contribution that Cuban psychology is making, compared to other Latin American psychologists (Molina Avilés 1986; Nydia Ramos and González Rey 1986) as well as maintaining a critical distance from bourgeois tendencies (Ortíz Torres et al. 1987).

Finally, the *Revista del Hospital Psiquiátrico de la Habana* (Journal of the Psychiatric Hospital of Havana) provides increased space for the publication of the results of experimental, interdisciplinary studies that show a sophisticated understanding of the relationship between issues of interest to psychologists and psychiatrists. For example, the semantic structures and vocabulary used by persons experiencing mental illness have been studied as cues to possible symptoms in the diagnosis and treatment of such disorders (Angel Calviño 1983; González Serra and Alonso Alvárez 1983). Another interesting study found that adolescent "transgressors" lacked a well-developed general conception of moral conduct typically acquired by normal youth of their age and that they were therefore unable to evaluate the consequences of their actions in terms other than those of personal gratification and self-interest (Roca Perara et al. 1982).

Cultural Barriers to Psychological Change

Since the revolution, psychologists have been challenged to develop a psychology that addresses needs and problems indigenous to Cuban culture but that also contributes to a socialist conception of persons. Uncertainty lingers as to what elements of Cuban culture persist after the revolution and whether there are legitimate forms of individual expression (i.e., rather than counterrevolutionary vestiges of bourgeois influences) embodying underlying and enduring psychological needs. Consequently, it is difficult to determine whether some Cubans are exhibiting neurotic or pathological reactions to the pressures of development and social transformation or are simply rejecting new regime values and expectations. This uncertainty of interpretation complicates the development of a socialist psychology, for if the very criteria used to define well-being are too demanding or unattainable, they may, in fact, contribute to resistance and evasion and produce neurotic symptoms that may require treatment. Moreover, an increased emphasis on preventive health policies may account for the recent acceleration of research in personality development, as such a policy presupposes that early intervention will not merely prevent negative behavior disorders but will also promote positive personality development—an assumption shared by U.S. psychologists that remains unproven.

The possibility that some of the goals and expectations for individual conduct in a socialist state may be too demanding (such as insisting that prerevolutionary culture be rejected) appears to have never been considered by Lourdes García-Averasturi, former head of the National Group in Psychology of the Ministry of Public Health. In describing the role of community health psychology in Cuba, García-Averasturi boldly asserts that after the revolution

> it became less important for psychologists to adapt people with emotional problems to living conditions impossible to change or to change behavior produced by a regimen of exploitation. Clearly, the societal transformation required for favorable change to occur in family, work, and social life had occurred already. Our function became one of contributing to and accelerating this transformation through our interventions as health workers in a new society. (1985:119)

However, this optimism may not be justified. One perspective thought to be characteristic of a society consciously pursuing modernization is a strong, nearly exclusive orientation toward the future. Nowhere is this future orientation more pronounced as official policy than in socialist countries embarked on a process of development toward an ideal communist society. This belief rationalizes the present sacrifices that citizens must endure to reach the "promised land."

Yet Cuban refugees from the Mariel boatlift interviewed by Cros-Sandoval (1986:54) had not internalized a futuristic orientation. Instead, they exhibited a marked orientation toward the present in which anxiety about what the future would bring placed a premium on getting by day to day. Mariel refugees also exhibited more of a subjugation orientation characteristic of so-called traditional, rather than modern, societies. Thus, instead of experiencing the shock of continued change, Cubans exhibited frustration with the complete predictability of daily life. Coping with sameness, according to Cros-Sandoval (1986:55), requires the cultivation of confused consciousness (*aturdirse*) whereby frustrations are purposely forgotten by erasing the uncanny but disturbing resemblance between one day and the next. Consequently, those psychologically unable to deceive themselves may be susceptible to depression or other psychosomatic disorders.

Next, prerevolutionary Cuban conscience was formed by the need to avoid impersonality in relationships. Cubans were judged primarily according to how they behaved toward friends and family rather than in terms of public life or performance in business. Personalization demands trust between two people in which acts of loyalty transcend all other obligations to the community and state. Consequently, overgenerousness is admired almost to a fault, and empathy and compassion are expected between friends, even if an individual does nothing right or deserves her or his own fate (Cros-Sandoval 1986:58–60). Cubans exhibit a proclivity to find extenuating circumstances that justify flaws in human character and a protective attitude such as is embodied in the diminutive ending— *ito*.

Paradoxical as it seems, Castro is viewed by some participants as embodying precisely the opposite values—considered virtues of personalism—such as rigidity, vindictiveness, distrust, and suspicion. For this reason Castro is widely admired and exalted, yet feared and despised. He is esteemed for exhibiting the traits of a caudillo, which include daring, unpredictability, cleverness, and boisterousness. Yet he is seen as lacking in some of the more humane and compassionate characteristics expected of a charismatic personality. This is not to say that Castro is not personable, as his closest friends attest. Rather, his cunning underscores his inability to make personal relationships occupy a non-strategic role in his life.

Castro is also not perceived as a family man or as capable of expressing himself in a sincere and compassionate manner. Yet Castro's most eloquent admirers contend that his struggle to overcome a self-indulgent marriage and a complacent family life constituted his greatest challenge in becoming, in Castro's words, "a man that is totally free" (Krich 1981). His impersonality and impartiality are believed to disguise a ruthlessness best captured by the phrase *El no cree en nadie* (He cares for nobody—nor stops at anything). His boldness is respected, but his domineering personality overwhelms opposition so that he *es el que mas dice* (always has the last word) (Cros-Sandoval 1986:64–66).

Yet those closest to Castro claim his personality is misunderstood. In a touching rejoinder to those who find fault with Castro's character, García Márquez (1990:46–47) writes that Castro has adopted techniques of improvisation, oratory, and interrogation, which sometimes appear overbearing and intolerant, in order to overcome a basic shyness with people. He is also consumed by a passion for detail and truth that no doubt makes others feel inadequate and defensive.

But perhaps the one element of revolutionary *conciencia* most inconsistent with prerevolutionary culture is that of conscientiousness. Cuban character is defined and judged less in terms of what a person does in work or career than by what attitude he or she assumes toward life and what feelings he or she expresses in relationships. The quality of being *simpático* often excuses character flaws that would otherwise not be tolerated (Cros-Sandoval 1986:62). Cuban individualism then is defined subjectively as a feeling of self-worth. This outlook on life is captured in its most extreme form by the expression *Ser como soy y quiero ser.* Cubans are what they want to be with little concern for future consequences.

Cuban author Edmundo Desnoes's book *Inconsolable Memories of Underdevelopment* (1967) exemplifies the feelings of ambivalence and dissonance that many Cubans experienced in their attempts to identify with or adapt to revolutionary changes that they only vaguely comprehended and understood. Desnoes (1967:52) attributes these feelings to an incapacity endemic to underdevelopment—that is, "an inability to relate things, to accumulate experience and to develop." The protagonist in Desnoes's novel (1967:37) confesses to trying to overcome the same weaknesses that he loathes in other Cubans: "their great incapacity to maintain a feeling, an idea, without scattering themselves." This contributes, according to Desnoes, to an incapacity to anticipate the future or to relate one's past to present conditions. That is why Desnoes's protagonist (1967:52) is critical of those unable to adjust to the sacrifices entailed in the revolutionary experience and complains that "whatever talent Cubans might have is wasted as they try to adapt to the present, to this very instant. Wasted on appearances. People are not consistent, they're satisfied with too little. Drop projects when they're half finished, interrupt their own feelings, fail to follow through to their final consequences."

In this regard, the *Boletín de Psicología* carried excerpts from Soviet psychologist Philip Bassin's book *The Problem of Inconsistency* in issues covering a period of three years from 1979 through 1982. Bassin explored a variety of factors that he believed contribute to inconsistency, such as complex and confusing tasks, poorly identified goals, unresolved emotional conflicts, weak attachments between members of a group, and low morale.

Psychology, Psychiatry, and Community Health Prevention

Psychology was not recognized as a separate discipline in the national university system until 1961, although professional training was provided in two private universities before 1959. At that time, psychology was given the status of a school within the faculty of science instead of the humanities or social sciences. Then, in 1976 psychology was recognized as an independent school with closer ties established with the social, rather than the natural, sciences (Bernal 1985:229; Marin 1988:140). As noted before, Cubans have relied heavily upon Soviet academicians for theoretical orientation and training of candidates pursuing doctorates in psychology. For example, in 1983 nearly one-third of the forty-three professors in the Department of Psychology at the University of Havana had obtained their Ph.D.s in the Soviet Union (Marin 1988:141). This close relationship is reflected in collaborative research undertaken between Cuban and Soviet psychologists reported in scholarly journals in psychology and other disciplines.

The general education requirements for a degree in psychology in Cuba resemble those in the United States. Students take courses in clinical and educational psychology, experimental and social psychology, and the psychology of work (Bernal 1985:229; Marin 1988:141). After five years of study, graduates are placed in a wide variety of settings, which include polyclinics, work centers, research institutes, schools, and hospitals. The Department of Psychology at the University of Havana maintains from 300 to 500 full-time-equivalent students and graduates 100 to 125 students per year (Bernal 1985:229). As of 1983 there were 18 doctoral candidates, with another 24 projected to complete their Ph.D. requirements by 1987 (Bernal 1985:231). García-Averasturi (1985:122) reports that in 1980, 310 psychologists and 350 psychometric technicians were distributed in 120 polyclinics, 44 hospitals, 10 research institutes, and other areas. The Society of Cuban Psychologists, headed by González Rey, was formed in 1981 to be a professional association for academics and psychologists working outside the Ministry of Public Health (Bernal 1985:232; Marin 1988:139).

Most psychologists work within the Ministry of Public Health. Ministry psychologists participate in a great variety of educational activities and conduct research and evaluations involving the delivery of health services (Marin 1988:138, 140). A significant number of psychologists also provide consultation and conduct research in the workplace. Their tasks include analyses of factors affecting worker motivation, such as the organization of work teams, training, processes of employee selection, and job development. In addition, social psychologists contribute to knowledge about the formation of community and group attitudes and social values, factors affecting professional role development, and institutional responsibilities and public opinion, among other subjects pertinent to social policy (Mitjans Martínez and Febles Elejaldes 1983). Finally, psychometricians help administer diagnostic tests, lead therapeutic discussion groups, and assist in collecting data for the Ministry of Public Health. García-Averasturi (1985:121) indicates that these technicians have helped psychologists undertake a more innovative and supportive role in community health psychology.

A division of labor has slowly emerged in the last two decades among psychologists, social psychiatrists, and epidemiologists. Hospital-based psychiatrists initially dominated diagnostic and therapeutic mental health services. However, the polyclinic made outpatient care feasible for patients experiencing less chronic mental disorders and neuroses. Nevertheless, physicians have resisted these changes (Pérez-Stable 1985:135) and have been reluctant or unwilling to refer patients to psychologists for assistance. For example, a random survey of eighty-seven physicians found that only 4 percent would send a patient to a clinical psychologist for a minor emotional disturbance (Marin 1985:152).

Patients also indicated that they initially sought help from friends, family, or a *curandero* or *curandera* (i.e., a follower of *Santería* or other religious cults) before seeking professional assistance and reported that they were most often referred to a psychiatrist (Camayd-Freixas 1985a:171), even when the problems were of a minor nature (Marin 1985:146). One probable reason for this reluctance is that persons suffering from psychiatric disorders are routinely brought to the attention of the CDRs by polyclinic staff, who assist in case-finding and follow-up functions. This network of community intervention, best described by its originator, Barriento Llano (1977), a psychiatrist, compromises confidentiality and thus discourages full use of polyclinic services (Camayd-Freixas and Uriate 1980:345, 350). Psychologists have experienced partial success in overcoming these limitations by offering group therapy, a mode of intervention that has shown a recent surge in popularity (Camayd-Freixas and Uriate 1980:345; Marin 1985:148). Since the mid-1980s, psychiatrists have limited their work to the rehabilitation of patients suffering from chronic mental disorders such as schizophrenia. They have innovated in techniques of "work therapy" designed to reintegrate persons suffering from dissociated cognitive or emotional states by completing progressively more complex tasks and responsibilities (Valdéz and Montalvo 1985).

Psychiatric social epidemiologists have assumed responsibility for the analysis of factors contributing to stress-related diseases such as arteriosclerosis and serious depressive and emotional disorders. Special areas of interest have included work-related causes of absenteeism and disabilities, the impact of work transfers and relocation, and the stress-related effects of participation in groups or enterprises (Camayd-Freixas 1985a:165). Significantly, Cuban epidemiologists attribute stress primarily to the effects of the scientific and technological revolution, which requires new forms of adaptation given the increased importance of communication and the "psychologization" of everyday life. Studies of situations involving rapid change have led these scientists to conclude that the rate of change is less disruptive than the perceived desirability of the change. For example, one study of the effects of relocation of residents of Villa Clara province found that satisfaction increased (and stress diminished) when the benefits of new living conditions became apparent. The idea that change is not necessarily perceived as threatening is consistent with Cuban psychological theory (see González Rey 1987), which holds that the capacity to maintain an objective and nonfearful attitude constitutes a critical factor in the formation of value judgments.

Organizational and Policy Advisory Role

Psychologists and psychiatrists first began to assume a significant role in health policy when the national groups in psychology and psychiatry were formed in 1968 to coordinate their respective professional activities within the provinces and localities. Significantly, these professional groups were formed in advance of the National Forum on Internal Order in 1969, making their preliminary evaluations of health and related social services available in the discussion of key problems affecting the stability of Cuban society. The leaders of these and other health-related professional groups form a national mental health group that participates in policymaking at the Ministry of Public Health (Camayd-Freixas and Uriate 1980:338). The roles of the two kinds of specialists in policymaking, however, are not equivalent. The National Group of Psychologists possesses the authority to evaluate and oversee the implementation of policies pertaining to all elements of the health-care delivery system (García-Averasturi 1985:287). The role of the National Group of Psychiatrists is limited to the development of professional standards and the coordination of the delivery of hospital-based psychiatric services to polyclinics (Camayd-Freixas and Uriate 1980:344).

A number of factors account for the National Group of Psychologists' significant role in public health policy, including a broad mandate, effective ties with mass organizations, and leadership support. Psychologists have defined their mandate to encompass the responsibility for the "well-being" of Cuban citizens. García-Averasturi (1988:286), former head of the national group, states more specifically that "the ultimate objective of public health psychology is to promote the development of individual potentialities and self-fulfillment throughout the life cycle (childhood, youth, adulthood, and old age), with all that this implies for health, longevity, and a feeling of well-being."

García-Averasturi (1988:296) claims that these objectives are tempered by the recognition that "psychological intervention can in no way take the place of the political will to improve living conditions and ways of life among different sectors of the population." Nevertheless, García-Averasturi (1988:296) believes that the application of psychological techniques will "contribute to speeding up the necessary changes in individual life style and personality" and that this "may exercise a positive influence on 'superstructural phenomena' such as values, customs and ideology including 'microsocial processes.'"

The attainment of a sense of well-being requires intervention to help the individual obtain self-fulfillment as well as to prevent behavior that may somehow undermine or interfere with the realization of her or his potential. Self-fulfillment occurs, according to García-Averasturi (1988:296), when individuals are able to control reality by "transforming adverse conditions" and "stressful situations," enabling "them to 'grow' in difficult situations" and feel a stronger motivation "for self care and the leading of a healthy life." This statement is striking in its recapitulation of logic of struggle first enunciated by Che Guevara, with his strong emphasis on the purifying and transformational effects of hardship and physiological stress.

González Rey (1988) has recently urged that psychologists, biochemists, and physicians collaborate in the interdisciplinary study of factors affecting the human immune reaction to stress. He believes that such a study would provide psychologists with invaluable insights regarding the psychobiological dynamics of stress and would generate techniques most likely to strengthen the body's resistance to emotional disorders and mental illness.

García-Averasturi (1988:287) contends that psychologists' success in influencing national policy in health care "depends *inter alia* on an ability to demonstrate the usefulness of the interventions." Positive personality development also requires the adoption of preventive measures, according to García-Averasturi (1988:285), that eliminate harmful habits and protect against other "dangerous forms of behavior." Although the distinction is not clearly drawn between intervention that promotes well-being and those influences undermining it, García-Averasturi (1988:286–87) suggests that preventive strategies be undertaken to implement legal mandates for well-being that attempt to influence the environment or institutional site (family, school, work) in which personality develops. A mandate conceived in these terms provides enormous discretion to determine the kind of intervention techniques considered appropriate and to decide how they will be used to define the limits of desirable and permissible behavior.

The organizational structure and administrative apparatus through which community mental health services are delivered provide additional leverage to psychologists to influence the implementation of social policy. The National Group of Psychologists prepares an annual action plan, which is transmitted to provincial and municipal affiliates, who then work out specific goals and activities to be implemented by polyclinics in collaboration with local OPP delegates and mass organizations (García-Averasturi 1988:290). Lowenthal et al. (1985:113) report that it is not uncommon for a psychologist to coordinate the activities of local CDRs.

All polyclinic psychological services in a municipality are supervised and evaluated by a "municipal psychology activist" chosen by local leaders but administratively accountable to provisional and ministry officials. This organizational structure promotes uniformity while enabling local experimentation. Psychological services offered through the polyclinic include diagnostic testing, educational and therapeutic interventions, special counseling for pregnant women, and treatment for children or adolescents suffering from behavioral disorders. Perhaps the most significant task assumed by psychologists is evaluating the effectiveness of the entire health team, including consumer perceptions of the quality of services. Psychologists also participate in interdisciplinary evaluations of health-related problems at work centers and in schools, which provide an important source of information as to the quality of health care and an impetus to policy changes initiated by the Ministry of Public Health (García-Averasturi 1985:120–21).

In 1984 the National Group of Psychologists launched a new statistical system that was expected to greatly enhance the quantity and quality of data pertaining to the operation of the health-care system (García-Averasturi 1988:293–94). The system focuses primarily on the nature and frequency of specialist consultations classified by type of problem and age of patient, reasons for seeking care, places visited, number of attending physicians including psychologists, type of treatment or test administered, and number of follow-up visits. This system also provides data to compare provinces in terms of the number and types of patients served, to determine the relative productivity of various specialists, and to gauge the adequacy of polyclinic linkages with mass organizations. Information of this kind is considered indispensable in determining not only whether the population is getting adequate health care but also whether physicians and psychologists are conscientiously fulfilling their responsibilities to prevent the onset of illness and nervous disorders. Feinsilver (1989b:86) found evidence that this system encourages doctors to schedule more frequent visits than is medically necessary in order to fulfill norms dictated by the Ministry of Public Health.

Another innovation Cuban psychologists introduced recently is an automated system for the retrieval of health records for use in the diagnosis of potential psychological factors contributing to somatic illnesses or disorders. The PSICOMET system enables the user (either the patient or psychologist) to combine neuropsychological indicators with the Minnesota Multiphasic Personality Inventory in order to determine whether specific physical symptoms may be associated with a particular psychological disorder (Gómez et al. 1989:6). PSICOMET is expected not only to enhance medical diagnoses but also to provide indicators to predict and thus prevent, for example, the onset of heart disease in type A personalities or the tendency toward suicide in persons suffering from depression. The system is intended to overcome the fear, anxiety, and reticence that prevent many people from seeking medical assistance. If confidentiality and privacy are safeguarded, then such reservations may be overcome. Nevertheless, such a system presupposes consensus, which does not now exist, on the etiology of psychosomatic disorders.

If proximity to Fidel Castro and other party leaders is an important criterion for assessing the power and influence wielded by subordinates, then psychologists and other specialists and scientists in human and social development appear to exercise a significant degree of influence by virtue of the role they play in the experimental and evaluation stages of the policymaking process outlined in Chapter 5. During these early stages expertise is sought to identify problems and establish objectives, to set programmatic contours, and to devise methods to implement and evaluate them in the field. An essential tool in gaining access to policymaking processes dominated by centralized planning and the one-party politics of unanimity is to possess expertise and techniques that will reduce uncertainty by increasing the capacity of decisionmakers to anticipate problems, predict reactions, and thus control the outcomes and consequences of policies.

Psychologists have adeptly fulfilled these requisites to policy influence by devising methods that enable the coordination of issues and problems that overlap and cut across policies and constituencies. For example, the psychological health and well-being of workers operating under the unrelenting burdens of the blockade, who are experiencing the anxiety of being idled by the special period, is essential to continued economic growth and productivity. The morale, motivation, and aspirations of students and youthful entrants into the work force must also be maintained at high levels in order to sustain their continued allegiance to a regime whose future depends upon continued struggle and sacrifice. Psychologists are helping Castro discover new ways he can project his influence beyond the limits of exhortation to sustain a will and a capacity in Cubans to struggle and resist capitulation to the inner voices of despair, dissension, and disillusionment.

7

Cuban Medicine: Health-Care Reform and the Revolution in Biotechnology

In a speech shortly after the Cuban rebel army marched victoriously into Havana in 1959, Che Guevara (a physician by training) saluted members of the Cuban Medical Federation in what at that time was surely more of a prophecy than a reality: "Of all the professions, it is the medical profession which has given most to the revolution" (Danielson 1979:128). At the onset of the revolution in 1960, Guevara provided a highly suggestive but unsystematic outline for the practice of social medicine. Castro probably did not fully grasp the psychobiological implications of Guevara's conception of social medicine at that time because he admitted to a complete lack of knowledge or understanding of the biological sciences (Betto 1987).

Under a system of social medicine, physicians would not be confined to hospitals but would be enlisted in a comprehensive investigation of every environmental, physical, and emotional factor affecting human well-being. The ecology of health care, according to Guevara (1968a:114), involved "the creation of a robust body with the work of the entire collectivity upon the entire social collectivity." Prevention consisted not only of the detailed compilation and analysis of diseases but also of a history of "what their sufferings are . . . including their chronic miseries for years, and what has been the inheritance of centuries of repression and total submission" (Guevara 1968a:115). Foreshadowing the enormous investment in Cuban medicine in the years ahead, Guevara (1968a:119) evoked a military metaphor to dramatize the conversion from guerrilla to medical tactics when he proclaimed, "Now the conditions are different, and the new armies which are being formed to defend the country must be armies with different tactics. The doctor will have an enormous importance within the plan of the new army."

The structure and function of the Cuban health-care system have evolved in many respects along the lines envisioned by Guevara. An enormous investment of resources and preventive programs that involve continual intervention have resulted in the allocation of 1 physician for every 302 inhabitants (as of 1991), with projected plans to attain an even greater level of coverage (Feinsilver 1989b:159).

In 1991 Cuba trained more than four thousand physicians (in 21 medical schools), who staff 422 polyclinics and 250 hospitals (Nelson 1991:33). Some distinguished visitors from the United States have been impressed with Cuban medical education, which emphasizes physiology and epidemiology (Bohr 1979). Feinsilver (1989a; 1989b) contends correctly that health and the quality of medical care have become primary symbols by which the Cuban regime and its citizens measure Cuba's legitimacy as a socialist state and prestige as an actor in world politics.

Cuba also exports health-care services to Third World countries. In 1980 approximately fifteen hundred physicians, or 13 percent of Cuba's twelve thousand national health service doctors, were providing health education and services to twenty countries in Africa and the Near East. By 1988 another twelve countries, many of which were purchasing sophisticated medical equipment, were receiving Cuban medical assistance (Santana 1990:262). In addition, as of 1985 Cuba had hosted eighteen hundred foreign students on medical scholarships from seventy-five Third World countries. Unlike U.S. foreign students, Cuban foreign medical students are required to return to their own countries after graduation (Feinsilver 1989a:15). The priority given health-care investments abroad contributes to Cuba's international prestige as a technically competent scientific world power (Feinsilver 1989a:24). Yet some physicians from the United States and other countries who have observed Cuban medicine are mystified by the seemingly inordinate resources devoted to health care and remain skeptical of the necessity to sustain such a huge commitment to medical care (Nelson 1991).

Castro has long considered improvements in health care to be a critical element in achieving international acceptance and respectability. Consequently, he is involved personally in almost every international health issue considered salient to Cuban interests. For example, in 1986 Castro hosted and addressed an international seminar on primary health care cosponsored by the World Health Organization (WHO) and the Pan American Health Organization (PAHO), which was headed that year by a Cuban physician (Granma Weekly Review 1986e). Castro has strongly supported WHO policies that define health as a positive state of complete physical, mental, and social well-being rather than merely as the absence of ill-health (Lambo 1985:75). WHO officials have reciprocated Castro's support by endorsing Cuba's biomedical research and by recently locating WHO's new Pan American headquarters in Havana—a move that will provide Cuba added leverage over international health policies (FBIS 1991h:12).

Castro's public discourse is now replete with frequent and so esoteric references to biomedical research that he believes will gu the survival of Cuba through the most ominous crisis yet to be raced since the early years of the revolution. However, the ongoing transformation of health care has been complex and controversial, involving investment priorities and health strategies that pose unknown hazards to the environment and uncertain consequences for individual rights.

This chapter examines key organizational and professional factors that have affected strategies to expand preventive health care in Cuba in the last three decades. Although the resources devoted to health care have increased enormously, these expenditures have not been altogether successful in implementing a preventive public health mission. The coordinated delivery of comprehensive health services has been fraught with difficulty, and physicians have been reluctant to adopt responsibilities that go beyond the realm of medical treatment. Advances in Cuban biomedicine show great promise in eliminating congenital defects and stress-related diseases, but the accelerated development and application of products of recombinant DNA research raise serious ethical and environmental issues that have yet to be adequately addressed by policymakers and the Cuban public.

The Polyclinic Health-Care Concept

The dramatic depletion of medical personnel resulting from the exodus of one-half of its sixty-three hundred physicians by 1963 forced Cuba to postpone implementing major changes in the service delivery system (Danielson 1979:131, 138–39). Health-care services were offered through existing "mutualist clinics," which provided comprehensive primary care to approximately 40 percent of the Cuban population (Danielson 1979:150–54). The shortage of doctors was handled by importing Soviet and other foreign physicians and by assigning all medical graduates to one year of rural service. By 1963 more than fifteen hundred physicians had performed this obligatory duty (Danielson 1979:133).

Cuban health officials initially attempted to copy the Czechoslovakian model of health planning, which combined "normative" centralization with an administratively decentralized delivery system. Party cadres initially used a heavy-handed approach to get physicians to accept the principles of socialist medicine. But this overly formalized effort to reeducate physicians about socialist objectives soon gave way to less antagonistic, more innovative methods. Regional task forces were established, pooling the knowledge of functionally related specialists likely to cooperate because they were involved in a preexisting pattern of collaboration through informal professional networks (Stein and Susser 1972:558).

Danielson (1979:148) contends that this method of reform accelerated the processes of administrative reorganization by giving medical specialists a stake in the positions they would occupy in the emerging national hierarchy of health officials.

These efforts resulted in the creation of the area polyclinic program in 1965. This health-care program sought to reduce the burgeoning demand for hospital services by expanding the availability of and access to primary health care in both rural and urban areas. It was designed to serve an average population of approximately twenty-five thousand people and to integrate four primary functions: clinical, environmental, community, and related social services. Polyclinic staff members were loaned by hospitals on a part-time basis and organized into teams of primary care specialists that included an internist, a pediatrician, an obstetrician-gynecologist, a dentist, a nurse, and a social worker. Polyclinics also coordinated their services with mass organizations such as the CDRs in conducting sanitation and immunization work in local communities (Danielson 1979:161–70; Pérez-Stable 1985:126). Thus, the polyclinic offered clinical outpatient services designed to prevent illness and to improve the quality of public health (Gilpin 1978).

Despite these initiatives, the polyclinic was still unable to realize its full potential, especially for preventive health care. An interdisciplinary assessment commission was appointed to bring health activities, including deficiencies in the polyclinic, under sharper administrative scrutiny (Danielson 1979:198; Pérez-Stable 1985:128). The commission was particularly interested in finding a way to free polyclinics from dependency on hospital resources and in expanding the role of psychologists in health care (Danielson 1979:196–97). The conflict between the centralizing tendencies of hospital inpatient services and decentralized outpatient services did tend to undermine the goals of the polyclinic concept. With their superior resources and specializations, hospitals still exercised dominant control over the distribution of medical personnel (Danielson 1979:190; Pérez-Stable 1985). Polyclinics had to be located near a hospital in order to get sufficient staff. This increased polyclinic dependency on hospitals for specialist assistance, which was uneven at best. For example, in 1974, 80 percent of medical school graduates reported that they still sought residencies in hospitals specializing in the treatment of acute illness and looked upon polyclinics as unprestigious assignments (Danielson 1979:190).

These negative attitudes about primary health care were typical of those found in other communist states. The general disdain that the public and physicians had for primary health care in Eastern European states such as Czechoslovakia was an almost insurmountable obstacle for former communist governments to overcome in providing adequate health care (Heitlinger 1991:211–12).

Other areas of patient dissatisfaction included overcrowding, long lines, superficiality of services, multiple referrals, substitutions of consultations, and inadequate follow-up. Most patients also criticized polyclinics for failing to assign each patient a doctor who would assume long-term responsibility for treatment and follow-up (Pérez-Stable 1985: 128–29). For these reasons, patients often bypassed polyclinics and initiated contact through hospital emergency rooms only when their medical problem was in an acute state, thus negating the value of prevention.

Finally, a significant problem reflected in patient criticisms was that physicians and nonphysicians were unable, and sometimes unwilling, to work effectively as a team. Little effort was made at systematic outreach, with case-finding tasks left largely to the CDRs (Pérez-Stable 1985:128–29). Team members rarely appeared at polyclinics at the same time and were often sidetracked by conferences with specialists at hospitals. Joint consultations were infrequent, and disagreement abounded when they did take place (Pérez-Stable 1985). Cleavages between specialists tended to form along functional lines: Psychologists sided with pediatricians, and psychiatrists supported the judgments of internists (Gilpin 1978:31).

Patients continued to complain about the quality of polyclinic services even after efforts had been made to improve services. A confidential public survey of complaints (whose authenticity is not questioned—see Feinsilver 1989b:250–51) was conducted by the Cuban Communist Party in 1988 in Holguín province to identify deficiencies in primary health care. One of the most common criticisms was the frequent absence or shortage of physicians or other supporting professional staff. Significantly, the percentage of unfavorable opinions involving this and other problems had increased an average of 3 percentage points (from 84.6 percent to 87.6 percent) since a 1986 survey (Cuban American National Foundation 1988:34). Other frequent criticisms included the shortage of medicine, breakdown of equipment, negligence in medical diagnoses and treatment, abusiveness or indifference to patients, excessive bureaucracy, and limited hours.

Perhaps the most onerous criticism of polyclinic staff was the perception of favoritism in patient access to medical treatment and the resentment of the privileges doctors enjoyed, such as flexible work schedules and discretionary use of polyclinic-assigned vehicles. A significant number of respondents also complained about the difficulty of obtaining appointments to see specialists and the long delays in being seen; respondents also noted many instances in which some patients had been seen ahead of others, even with waiting rooms full of patients with previously scheduled appointments. Disparities in appointment scheduling were sometimes explicitly attributed to *sociolismo*—a doctor's friends or professional associates got special treatment. Long delays were explained by physician understaffing and the overreliance on nonphysician technicians for diagnostic and treatment services. Decree Law 113 was promulgated in 1989 to establish professional standards for physicians and to specify conduct that would result in disciplinary proceedings.

Consumer complaints such as those expressed in Cuba about the quality of and access to medical care were expressed in the Soviet Union (and in post-Gorbachev Russia, where the health-care system is considered a national disgrace) as well as in most other Eastern European states. Field (1991a:83) reports, for example, that health care in the Soviet Union was not a budget priority and that this legacy of this condition is reflected in the poor coverage of primary care and the low status accorded to medicine and health-related professions (Field 1991b:58–59). In addition, Field (1991a:86) found evidence of a two-tiered health system: a territorial network based on residency available to the general population and a special, closed network consisting of much-higher-quality specialist care reserved for various elite occupational groups and party members. In contrast, the Cuban medical profession generally is held in high esteem by Cubans, and no evidence has been found thus far of a dual system of health care.

The Matanzas Experiment and Community Medicine

The health-care system was viewed as a critical element of an overall plan to create a permanent structure of political and administrative decisionmaking for the delivery of social services at the provincial and community level. Significantly, the Matanzas experiment in *poder popular*, begun in 1974, was headed by Dr. Machado Ventura (Danielson 1979: 193), former minister of public health and current member of the Politburo, who, as noted in Chapter 5, has recently acquired control over all ministries concerned with domestic policy. Machado Ventura commissioned members of the National Group of Psychologists and the Cuban Society of Health Psychologists (formed in 1974) to evaluate the effectiveness of decentralizing administrative control of health and other social services.

The Matanzas experiment brought about several changes in the polyclinic concept under the rubric of "medicine in the community." Polyclinic teams were assigned to a specific sector or geographic population for primary care. In addition, target populations were defined according to high-risk groups such as infants and the elderly so that medical services could be dispensed to those in greatest need. Nevertheless, other changes reflected a deference to expertise that undermined these principles. For example, a generalist approach to health care and community prevention was countered by a concession that allowed physicians to limit their professional responsibility to only those health problems covered by their specialization. In addition, the attempt to increase specialist consultation with polyclinic staff simply reinforced polyclinic dependency on hospital-based physicians, thus unnecessarily prolonging the length of time involved in providing treatment.

Once again, the performance of the health-care system had fallen far short of expectations, which was due less to inadequacies in clinical services than to the inability to effectuate changes in physician roles consistent with a prevention-oriented mission. As evaluations completed by psychologists in the early 1980s made clear, the "medicine in the community program" was not working as intended. Specialists continued to work independently of one another, failed to establish contact with mass organizations and community leaders, and, most significantly, were unwilling to incorporate psychological and social factors in the diagnosis of health problems. Psychologists have conducted a number of studies examining factors thought to influence physicians' role perceptions and their willingness to adopt new perspectives toward patients and health. For example, Cuban psychologists have identified beliefs and attitudes motivating students to pursue a medical degree (Cura Morales 1983), analyzed differences in moral ideals held by medical students pursuing primary and secondary fields of specialization (Gozá León and Gutiérrez López 1986), and attempted to identify educational and achievement standards for students opting to specialize in medicine (González Menéndez 1984).

Following the lead of Soviet psychological theorists such as B.V. Zeigarnik and V.V. Nicolaeva (1981), whose work was published in the *Boletín de Psicología*, Cuban psychologists have suggested how physicians could incorporate knowledge of psychobiology in family medicine (Méndez Martínez et al. 1986). Psychosomatic factors have been identified in the diagnosis, treatment, and/or prevention of patients suffering from coronary ailments (Lauzurique Hubbard et al. 1983; Peña Bentancurt et al. 1987), bronchial asthma, and ulcers (Goza León 1982); and experimental attempts have been made to alter the onset of some diseases (ISCM-H. 1981). In addition, psychologists have assessed the importance of knowledge of personality development in clinical medical education (Veitía Mora et al. 1984).

One other factor considered crucial to the success of the family doctor program is the analysis of doctor-patient relationships. The lack of continuity between doctor and patient caused by the transient and episodic nature of health interventions constitutes a significant obstacle to a system of preventive health. The family doctor program is intended to overcome this problem, in part, by lowering the doctor-patient ratio sufficiently to make possible (theoretically) a prevention and treatment strategy to handle the actual or potential health problems of each individual living within the doctor's primary-health-care jurisdiction. Psychologists have suggested ways to increase physician sensitivity to and skills in conversing with patients (Sección Estudiantil 1982) so that a more permanent relationship can be forged between them (Gozá León 1983). This includes the capacity to overcome fear, distrust, and even the contempt that many patients have of health-care workers, which prevents them from seeking medical assistance (Uria et al. 1984).

Perhaps the most disheartening finding about the health-care system was that the polyclinic health team did not really know very well the characteristics of the population it was intended to serve (Santana 1987:116–17). Each polyclinic was issued a "red book" that provided a detailed statistical health profile of its community and supplied the norms and guidelines by which the community health profile could be updated and analyzed by the staff. However, as Feinsilver (1989b:68–69) reports, community health data were not employed in any systematic or integrated way. Moreover, the health profile of the population had undergone changes, which resulted in health problems that were not effectively detected by the polyclinic team. Many of the chronic illnesses that afflict older people with long latency periods, such as heart disease or cancer, were not adequately detected, and thus prevented, because of the insufficient morbidity data collected by polyclinic staff (Díaz Briquets 1983:118–19; Santana 1987:117).

The Politics of Public Health

One of the more curious aspects of preventive health education in Cuba is that it has actually increased patients' dependency on the physician. During the first decade of the revolution, most public health education campaigns were conducted by volunteers of the CDRs and the FMC. Their efforts were largely focused on sanitation, hygiene, and prevention of contagious diseases. CDR members were noteworthy for their work in community sanitation programs, and the FMC gained widespread notoriety for organizing the first nationwide vaccination for tetanus and polio and for providing staff for the burgeoning number of day-care centers where mothers received instruction in hygiene and maternal care.

The advent of professionalization of health care in Cuba has not so much displaced volunteers and community health workers as it has redefined and subordinated their mission within the health-care hierarchy. For example, *brigadistas sanitarias*, or members of health brigades, are trained to recognize symptoms of a few common diseases but are not entrusted to dispense other than the most rudimentary services or assistance to patients suffering from acute or chronic problems. Independent judgment is discouraged, as are emergency interventions that may have lifesaving consequences. This deference to expertise is encouraged among patients as well. For example, Dr. David Werner (1980:23) was incredulous that so little diagnostic information or explanations were provided to help an individual solve his or her health problems. When a polyclinic physician was queried about this apparent oversight, he replied, "We don't want to tell mothers anything that might lead them to put off getting adequate medical attention at once" (Werner 1980:24). This kind of attitude is exhibited in the abstruse and obfuscating language that adorns much health literature, further limiting its accessibility.

The quality of Cuban health care cannot be measured accurately solely by the physician-to-population ratio without taking into account the overall priorities served by a national investment in medicine. Cuban leaders expect a massive investment in physician training to offset its national trade debt through the export of physicians abroad and the sale of pharmaceutical products derived from advances in biomedical research (Feinsilver 1989b:119). Priorities such as these divert considerable resources and talent away from alternative domestic uses. Moreover, a commitment to public health must be measured by the willingness and capacity to implement environmental safeguards and educational strategies that enlist communities and individuals in the elimination of factors contributing to infectious and chronic diseases. Cuba's response to the dengue epidemics in 1977 and 1981, and its approach to reducing the incidence of smoking-related diseases, is indicative of the weaknesses of a physician-dominated public health infrastructure.

Cuba's handling of the dengue epidemic is singled out as an example of the effectiveness of mass participation in successfully ending a threat to public health. Dengue hemorrhagic fever is a highly contagious viral disease spread by mosquitoes. The dengue epidemic hit Cuba in 1981, hospitalizing more than 116,000 people (mostly children from ages one to fifteen) and killing 152 persons (101 children and 51 adults) before it was brought under control four months later (Kouri et al. 1989). Castro blamed the United States for introducing the virus, leading Feinsilver (1989b:128) to observe that the "dengue campaign epitomizes the intersection of symbolic politics and health and the symbolic war between Cuba and the United States."

Nevertheless, there is some evidence to suggest that the epidemic could have been prevented had Cuban health officials undertaken precautionary measures after a previous, less extensive outbreak in 1977. For example, a serological examination conducted by public health officials determined that more than five-hundred thousand people had been exposed to the disease in 1977, concluding that most of these persons would be at risk to a secondary infection if a different serotype was introduced (Kouri et al. 1989:375). Had Cuban health officials implemented sanitation measures and attempted to eradicate mosquito breeding grounds after 1977 instead of waiting until after 1981 to do so, then some of the $53 million (and lives) probably could have been saved.

The enormous investment that the Cuban leadership is making to find effective surgical interventions or drug treatments for chronic illnesses such as cancer, contagious diseases such as meningitis and hepatitis, and more exotic congenital and neural defects may enhance Cuba's image as a world class medical power, but this action does little to alter pathogenic environments and behaviors conducive to illness and mortality. Tesh (1986:97–98; 1988) reports that Cuba publishes no official statistics on occupational diseases, disseminates scanty information on disease-causing toxic substances, and only belatedly has provided clinical services in occupational medicine. There is also a conspicuous absence of a systematic educational campaign against the hazards of smoking, dietary and other causes of heart disease, and lung cancer. Tesh (1986:101) was told that Cuban health officials were opposed to individualizing a problem that required a collective solution. Perhaps this orientation accounts for an essential weakness in strategies predicated on a collective response: No change can occur unless everyone agrees to implement the same solution simultaneously. However, a more effective approach to weaknesses in health prevention will ultimately require a change in the attitudes physicians have about how they practice medicine.

The Family Doctor:
Social Medicine or Social Control?

The completion of a two-year interdisciplinary survey begun in 1980 to examine the quality and focus of university medical education in Cuba (Granma Weekly Review 1982:1, 3) convinced Castro and officials in the Ministry of Public Health that the structure of medical education needed fundamental revision. Consequently, the Carlos F. Finlay Medical Sciences Detachment was formed in 1982. This unit reflects Castro's attempt to alter how students are recruited and admitted to medical school. Castro acknowledged that the selection process for candidates for medical training had been haphazard, with little attention devoted to considerations beyond those pertaining to academic achievement. He was particularly irritated by the discovery that many students had chosen medicine as a second or third option and that they had generally ignored or avoided the field of social medicine (Granma Weekly Review

1982:3). Consequently, Castro saw the detachment as a way to screen and recruit high school seniors who exhibited the kind of attitude worthy of the privilege of receiving a medical education or, for that matter, professional training in any field of study.

The Finlay Medical Sciences Detachment and the family doctor program, begun in 1985, represent key elements of the regime's strategy to restructure the profession of medicine. The family doctor program is being wielded as a tool to influence the structure of Cuban medicine, particularly through the control of specialization. It provides Castro and PCC officials increased leverage over three of the most important factors governing the practice of medicine: admission standards, curriculum, and opportunities for specialization and advancement. In fact, family medicine was cleverly announced (Granma Weekly Review 1986a:4) as a new specialty and was subsequently designated as "integrated general medicine," thus eliminating the distinction between the practice of general medicine and specialization. Moreover, members of the detachment must obtain a degree in integrated general medicine before specializing in other areas.

The practice of family medicine in Canada experienced a resurgence after a national health insurance program was adopted that emphasized preventive primary health care. Approximately one out of every two medical students goes into family medicine, a field held in high esteem by physicians and the public (Walsh 1992:18). Cuba expects to match, if not eventually surpass, the proportion of doctors practicing family medicine in Canada. Of the three thousand doctors who graduate from medical school each year, more than half are expected to practice family medicine, most of whom will have entered school through the Finlay Medical Sciences Detachment. This figure contrasts sharply with the number of physicians practicing family medicine in the United States, which has declined 19 percent since 1986 (Walsh 1992:1). In 1989 only 11.7 percent of those completing medical school in the United States intended to go into family medicine (Walsh 1992:1).

Castro predicted that by 1996 there would be twenty thousand family doctors distributed among four hundred sites located in work centers, at schools, and on international missions to form a vast network of health services (Granma Weekly Review 1986a:4). As of 1988, 6,057 family doctors were providing medical services to more than 4 million people in agricultural coops, schools, work centers, and homes for the aged (Feinsilver 1989b:178–79). Approximately 75 percent of the family doctors were located in urban, rather than rural, areas. Feinsilver (1989b:159) reports that in 1987 there were 28,060 doctors in Cuba, or 1 for every 367 persons. She estimates that by the year 2000, Cuba will have 1 doctor for every 196 inhabitants, exceeding its own medical needs as well as outstripping the projected physician-to-population ratio in the United States of 1 to 405 (Feinsilver 1989b:159).

When Castro first introduced the family doctor concept in 1986, he expected it to implement more than a health mission. In his closing remarks to a convention of CDR members, Castro declared that the family doctor was intended not only to strengthen disease prevention but also to encompass the prevention of crime and delinquency. Castro underscored the importance of "medical social work" by noting that

> these doctors do good work and I know that it goes as far as crime prevention, because they're working with youngsters going astray, organizing them, channelling them into sports. So their work is going to be very helpful in crime prevention, in eliminating factors that go to make delinquents. These doctors know where their patients live and what their living conditions are like. The doctor in the polyclinic or hospital doesn't know how a family, person, or patient lives, but those at the grassroots level are really the committees for the defense of health, and they will be closely associated with you because they're organized the same way the Committees for the Defense of the Revolution are. (Granma Weekly Review 1986b:4)

These remarks suggest that the family doctor has been enlisted, in part, to penetrate the contrivances of ill-health that disguise truant and delinquent behavior so that intervention can occur. For example, one of the most frequently expressed concerns of those surveyed in Holguín province was the long delay in obtaining health certificates from family doctors that are generally issued to excuse absences for health reasons (Cuban American National Foundation 1988:3). Castro also expects the collaboration between doctors and the YCL to provide a mechanism for integration of family doctors into the Communist Party.

The family doctor health program began on an experimental basis in Havana. It was intended to overcome many of the deficiencies of the polyclinic concept by pursuing the following objectives: (1) to improve the health consciousness of the population, (2) to promote active participation in health services, (3) to achieve a close working relationship between physicians and the population, and (4) to increase trust in the health system by its users (Santana 1990:254). These physicians are expected to live within the community and provide preventive, curative, and environmental health services for approximately 600–700 people or approximately 120 families. The doctor's medical practice is begun by conducting an epidemiological diagnosis of the population that presents general information about the scope and distribution of health problems, including the physician's personal observations about those at risk for illness, disease, or social or psychological disorders. This information is then presented to a general assembly of residents. Having accomplished this, the doctor and community are able to proceed with health intervention from a common point of departure (Santana 1990:254).

The scope of the family doctor's responsibilities are extensive, going beyond purely medical activities to include assistance and follow-up over time of the "natural, social and economic factors influencing families' lives" (Granma Weekly Review 1986b:4). As such, Castro defined the family doctor program as a form of "medical social work": In other words the doctor will look after a pregnant woman, follow the evolution of her pregnancy and the period after delivery, follow the growth of the child, his psychomotor development and his behavior at school and later, when he grows up and goes to work, how he acts at work and in the family" (Granma Weekly Review 1986b:4).

Clearly, the family doctor's role is not limited to the prevention of disease or illness. Rather, it encompasses the continual collection of longitudinal data on the growth and well-being of every resident from birth to old age. As Santana (1987:118) observes, "The data bases generated by such a system could be an epidemiologist's dream, providing information about diseases and risk factors on a population basis." The value of data of this kind goes beyond their obvious utility in research and experimentation about the causes and potential treatment of disease. As Castro conceives it, these data are being collected in order to "make optimum use of human resources" (FBIS 1991a:10). Health is defined not just by the absence of disease but also by the capacity to be productive. Knowledge about environmental and genetic factors that interfere with good health can be converted through research in biomedicine into pharmaceutical products and technologies that alter the characteristics of the human organism.

It is not possible to evaluate definitively the effectiveness of these reforms in Cuban medicine because that requires data about the long-term effects of heath-care interventions. Castro claimed, without furnishing evidence, that family doctors had reduced hospital admittances (ironically an objective that the polyclinics were expected to achieve) and that many people had even stopped going to polyclinics (FBIS 1991a:8). However, little data are available thus far to gauge family doctors' impact on rates of morbidity and mortality. Recent statistics indicate, for example, that mortality rates resulting from infectious or diarrheal diseases had leveled off by 1980 (Limonta Vidal and Padrón 1991:104). Also, six of eleven of the leading causes of death actually increased between 1980 and 1988 (Limonta Vidal and Padrón 1991:105). Nor is it possible to gauge the reactions of users of family doctor services or to determine the attitudes and behavior of physicians enlisted to provide them until the results of future studies and surveys become available.

The reorganization of medical care in Cuba reflects the Cuban regime's attempt to harness the medical profession in the service of social control well beyond that necessary to meet acceptable standards of individual health. This is not to deny that the effort to prevent the onset of specific health problems and physical disorders is a legitimate and worthy enterprise. However, a program involving collaboration between party organs and physicians to obtain comprehensive longitudinal health and behavioral profiles that compromises confidentiality between doctor and patient, and invades privacy and jeopardizes personal integrity, may undermine confidence in and use of the family doctor program.

Biotechnology and Social Development

Cuba's commitment to biomedical research has been guided by the need to generate biotechnologies capable of solving pressing social and economic problems of development. The depth of this commitment is best illustrated in Castro's slogan adorning many laboratories: "The future of our country must of necessity be the future of men of science" (Ubell 1983a:745). Castro once characterized scientists who work devotedly and tirelessly for long hours as the "priests and nuns of science" who work in the "monasteries of biotechnological research" he has built for them—where, he rhetorically added, other workers might be "inoculated" against resistance to hard work (FBIS 1986:12). The crisis of survival Cuba now faces during the special period has increased the urgency to find immediate applications of scientific discoveries to production and society. Consequently, Castro promises that each time a scientific discovery is made, not even twenty-four hours will be lost before it is immediately applied to production (Granma Weekly Review 1991). Moreover, toward this end the Cuban government is building self-contained communities to house teams of scientists and their families involved in high-priority research in biotechnology (FBIS 1991i).

An indispensable factor contributing to the rapid development of Cuba's biomedical research establishment is the extraordinary success Castro and Cuban scientists have had in obtaining technical assistance from innovative experts in the field. For example, Castro's interest in cancer research was stimulated by consultation with Dr. Randolf Clark (1973), an oncologist and head of the University of Texas Cancer Research Center (FBIS 1986:8; Mina 1991:188–89). Castro's decision to produce leukocyte alpha interferon for cancer research and other biomedical uses was made possible by Dr. Karl Cantell, a Helsinki scientist who instructed Cuban scientists on how to manufacture it (FBIS 1986; Ubell 1983a:747). Other contacts occurred as a result of Cuba's unsuccessful competition for funding from the United Nations Industrial Development

Organization (UNIDO) to build a center for biotechnology and genetic engineering. Although the project was eventually divided between India and Italy (Sasson 1988:335), UNIDO helped Cuba finance a pharmaceutical plant to manufacture products of biogenetic research and since then has provided more than $11 million to support twenty other research projects in biotechnology. Cuba eventually built its own research center with astonishing speed largely because of expert assistance from Dr. Albert Sasson (1984), a French scientist with UNESCO whose book on biotechnology strongly influenced Castro's thinking and was distributed widely among Cuban scientists (FBIS 1986:7).

The areas of research that Cuba's National Center for Scientific Research (CNIC), first established in 1965, has chosen to support in biomedicine and biotechnology provide important clues about the aims, scope, and potential human consequences of the center's scientific program. The CNIC has given a relatively high priority to research in biomedicine that yields basic knowledge about neurophysiological factors influencing (either by promoting or retarding) human growth processes (see Chapter 4). One of the first spin-offs of CNIC-sponsored brain research was the national program in clinical neurophysiology. This program was started as a result of a collaboration with Cuban neurologists that was initiated in 1972 by Dr. E. Roy John (1977:xx), a neuroscientist from New York University, to explore the diagnostic applications of brain wave research. The Cuban scientists published several articles documenting the results of initial clinical trials (see, for example, Harmony et al. 1973a; 1973b), and new applications from ongoing research continue to be documented (Gevins and Rémond 1987). Dr. John and his colleagues (1988:168–69) contend that brain electrical activity, involving the interaction of neuroanatomical and neurochemical processes, displays a remarkably predictable pattern in normal people. However, this pattern is disrupted in persons suffering from nervous disorders, such as depression or schizophrenia, leaving a distinctive signature that can be used to diagnose and properly treat psychiatric illnesses. Diagnostic judgments are not foolproof, however, because there are often only slight differences between normal and abnormal brain wave patterns, which consequently require subjective interpretation.

Cuban neuroscientists have gone beyond psychiatric uses of neurometrics, such as that involved in diagnosing manic-depression (Reyes Gutiérrez and Simón Consuegra 1987), to examine its potential in diagnosing mental retardation and in assessing biorhythmic signs of potential fetal defects (Gonzáles Delgado 1983). The CNIC has created a network of laboratories in fourteen provinces dedicated to neuropediatrics, educational testing, and adult neuropsychiatry; these laboratories employ equipment developed to measure brain waves and detect audiovisual problems and perceptual impairment. From 1985 to 1989, 97.3 percent of all newborns were screened for auditory defects (Limonta Vidal and Padrón 1991:107). In addition, by 1988, 91.1 percent of all women had been tested for neural tube defects (4,258 cases had been detected) using an immunochemical reagent supplemented by electroencephalograms (Limonta Vidal and Padrón 1991:110).

Although the benefits of early detection derived from these diagnostic screening devices are commendable, it remains unclear how this alone explains or justifies the rather excessive amount of pre- and postnatal testing and examinations in comparison to other socialist states. For example, pregnant women in Cuba must schedule biweekly visits to an obstetrician (Nikelly 1987:123), compared to nine visits throughout the entire pregnancy in China (Chao 1984:221). Newborns are even separated from mothers and placed under observation and examined for up to twelve hours (Werner 1980:27). Infants must also be examined by a pediatrician twice a month for the first two years (Nikelly 1987:123). In addition, any eleven- or twelve-year-olds who experience school-related problems or delinquency must receive a complete psychological and neural diagnostic examination (Kates 1987:757). In China, by contrast, infants under one year of age are examined every three months, and one- to three-year-olds checked every six months (Chao 1984:233). The Chinese also rely more heavily on the judgment of laypersons, parents, and police in assessing the psychological disposition of and establishing the appropriate treatment for delinquent youth (Rojek 1989:94).

One explanation for extensive diagnostic examinations in Cuba, beyond obvious benefits in preventive health, is that they provide a source of natural control groups with which to experimentally test and assess the effectiveness of biomedical drugs and technologies generated from laboratory experimentation. Castro acknowledges that researchers are studying the effects on human subjects of medicines created through recombinant DNA techniques (FBIS 1991a:13). For example, interferon was administered experimentally with some success to children afflicted by the dengue virus in 1981 (Limonta Vidal and Padrón 1991:106–7). Cuban doctors are also treating with interferon Russian children who were exposed to radiation from the Chernobyl nuclear power disaster. Even Castro disclosed recently that he is taking a drug called "PPG," created in Cuba's biotechnological laboratories, which he claims lowers cholesterol and blood pressure, relieves circulatory problems, increases memory, and accounts for his unlimited energy (Schlesinger 1992).

Castro's personal interest in and strong commitment to biotechnology as a source of Cuba's economic salvation are well illustrated in his involvement in the Center for Biological Research (CIB), established in 1982, and the Center for Genetic Engineering and Biotechnology (CIBG), formed in 1986. During their short existence, the CIB and CIBG have produced more than 130 different products, which include 40 types of monoclonal antibodies with immunological applications in biomedicine. These centers are autonomous and function completely outside the control of the Academy of Sciences and the university system. Instead, they are accountable to a high-level policymaking body Castro formed in 1981 called the "Biological Front," which is responsible for establishing research priorities and approving applications of new products (Ubell 1983a:747). Castro, who is both knowledgeable and opinionated about appropriate biotechnological applications, relies heavily on the advice of this small advisory group of scientists, who monitor and evaluate research in biotechnology and other fields (Ubell 1983a:748).

The CIBG staff has sponsored or attended several seminars and international congresses on biotechnology, which have been devoted primarily to promotion of new products and applications of interferon (Feinsilver 1989b:222–26), but the staff lacks the kind of continual peer group review and scrutiny that come from refereed publication in respected international scientific journals. Although scientific visitors consider Cuba's research in genetic engineering to be ambitious and impressive, some express reservations about the advisability of the gamble Cuban scientists have made to use alpha interferon as the basis for the treatment of infectious diseases and immunological research (Beckwith 1985; Miller 1986). Interferon may not be the effective drug it was once touted to be, and biogeneticists are finding potentially more effective alternatives.

Other research centers have spun off from the CIBG. In 1987 the Center for Immunoassay (CEI) was created to develop diagnostic techniques based on immunochemical methodology. The CEI has manufactured a reagent (called SUMA) used to detect neural tube defects and other congenital abnormalities. SUMA is also being used to screen newborns for hyperthyroidism, a defect that disrupts weight gain associated with normal growth. In addition, more ambitious plans are being made to use SUMA to screen for leprosy and viral and parasitic diseases, with the goal of eventual eradication of these diseases (Limonta Vidal and Padrón 1991:110). This will undoubtedly increase the number of postnatal examinations already performed and will lead to the introduction of additional drugs produced through recombinant processes, which pose risks with uncertain human consequences.

Yet another center was established in 1989 dedicated to the interdisciplinary study of nervous system disorders. Scientists at the Center for Neurotransplants and Regeneration of the Nervous System conduct experimental neurosurgery to correct congenital or disease-related dysfunctions such as Parkinson's disease and spinal cord lesions.

Neurotransplantation of fetal brain tissue in adult patients is a relatively new field in Cuba, one fraught with controversy in the United States, that shows some promise in helping stroke victims toward partial recovery from functional paralysis. And, finally, the National Institute of Oncology and Radiobiology has been in operation since 1989, working specifically on the production of monoclonal antibodies for the diagnosis and treatment of cancer.

Cuban physicians and bioscientists have chosen to focus, among other areas, on the early diagnosis and treatment of neural, hormonal, and other growth-related congenital disorders because they expect to deepen their knowledge of the neurochemical processes regulating growth and the functioning of the immune system. They seek to discover the conditions under which cellular growth dysfunctions occur, as in the case of fetal development or cancer, in order to develop new monoclonal antibodies and related technologies that increase the body's capacity to resist stress and handle uncertain and risky situations with increased effectiveness. These explorations on the frontiers of biomedical knowledge about the human capacity for resistance simply reaffirm the thread of continuity that links Guevara's attempt to create a new person with the ongoing struggle to resist being constrained by limits such as those posed by U.S. hostility, disease, or fears and doubt.

Part 4

Conclusion and Assessment

8

Understanding Cuban Strategies for Social Development

As the previous chapters suggest, the processes of social development in Cuba have not conformed to a unilinear path toward modernization as measured by the yardstick of Western democracies, nor have they rigidly adhered to a course dictated by Marxist-Leninist theory whereby social and political practices are determined solely by economic relationships and structures. Instead, Cuban social policies and institutions have evolved through strategic experimentation with different programs and techniques in an ongoing struggle to implement a vision of a new person and a more just social order.

Nevertheless, the course of social development in revolutionary Cuba cannot be neatly separated from the turbulent international arena in which it has unfolded. The unabated U.S. hostility and economic block-ade, years of economic dependency on and political conflict with the Soviet Union, the dilemma of diversification in a sugar monoculture, and the changing structure of the world economy have each affected the choice and effectiveness of strategies of social development in significant ways.

The Cuban leadership has also encountered a great variety of unantic-ipated difficulties and resistance to policies intended to address common social problems that intersect different institutions and societal interests. For example, strategies of legal mobilization and redistribution were used to accelerate the processes of socialist development when new eco-nomic structures and governance processes were incipient and uncertain. These policies generated a number of social and economic costs (e.g., family instability, delinquency, labor unrest, and low productivity) that contributed to the adoption of new strategies of institutionalization and regulation in the 1970s and 1980s. An overcentralized and chaotic plan-ning and administrative structure was replaced with a constitutionally mandated system of national and local governance, widening the scope of participation in the allocation and use of goods and services. National laws and administrative codes were also adopted to prescribe the rights and enunciate the responsibilities that youth, workers, and families were expected to fulfill in contributing to the attainment of social development objectives.

A significant feature of the transition in strategies over time has been the increased involvement of physicians, psychologists, sociologists, and other professionals in the generation and implementation of social policy. The well-being of Cuban citizens is now being defined broadly by psychologists and physicians to encompass the prevention of emotional or physical illnesses that destabilize families and contribute to deviations from the processes of normal development. Although this trend has not displaced the leadership of party cadres or mass organizations, it has introduced a competing source of influence in policy implementation processes by placing increased emphasis on information, expertise, and techniques in problem solving.

In this chapter I put these factors in an analytical perspective that remains sensitive to the unique circumstances influencing Cuban development while enabling us to generalize about the processes that Cuba has undergone in realizing its objectives of social development compared to those experienced by other socialist countries. This analysis explains why Cuban strategies of social development have become intertwined with Cuba's foreign policy objectives, accounts for why the strategies and techniques have changed over time, and examines how issue networks have emerged to provide professionals increased leverage over policies governed by cadre-dominated clientism and informal exchange networks. In addition, I assess Cuba's prospects of overcoming the economic difficulties, political constraints, and social resistance that continue to block the path to complete social reconstruction.

The International Dimensions
of Cuban Development

Among the many external challenges that Cuba has faced in attempting to defend its revolution, perhaps no other factor has been more important than the U.S. blockade. The maintenance and gradual tightening of economic sanctions have severely constrained the choices and leverage that Cuban leaders have had in sustaining economic growth and competitiveness in the world economy. No other member states of the former communist bloc, including China and Vietnam, have had to withstand, as Cuba has, such a concerted and persistent effort by the United States to undermine a country's capacity to effectively engage in international trade. Cuba has paid an incalculably high price for a U.S. policy that was originally designed to penalize Cuban foreign adventurism but that now seems to be driven by little more than vindictiveness and ideological dogma.

By the same token, however, it would be highly misleading to argue that the Cuban strategies for social development described in this book have been either dictated by Soviet advisers or undertaken in response to pressure from the United States. For example, if the hypothesis were true that Cuban social policies have been induced by continual U.S. pressure and threats, then it would be difficult to explain why the CDRs' mission has changed from maintaining vigilance against foreign invasion or sabotage to controlling and preventing crime. Nor can the transition from punitive to preventive approaches to social order be explained somehow as a response to U.S. hostilities. Instead, the different policies that have emerged appear to have been the result of endogenous problems and conflicts unavoidably entailed in the processes of revolutionary social change.

To be sure, Castro has frequently cynically exploited U.S. hostility to justify policies that otherwise lack support, but that does not mean that they would not have been undertaken in the absence of U.S. pressure. In many ways, Cuban nationalism bears the marks (or scars) of a long-term conflictual relationship with the United States, and Cuba's identity is bound up in the continuation of this oppositional relationship. Moreover, I do not believe that normalization of U.S.-Cuban relations would change Cuba's conception of its leadership role in international development policy, nor would normalization diminish the differences that set these two nations apart in their ideological and strategic approaches to issues of world economic development.

Cuban leaders have achieved some limited success in getting the international community in the United Nations to debate and condemn the U.S. embargo. They also have enlisted the support of several U.N. organizations in condemning U.S. economic sanctions on moral grounds. There is no question that Cuba's medical assistance to people of impoverished Third World countries has greatly enhanced its prestige in U.N. circles. Cuba's plight has generated increased sympathy from Third World nations disaffected with the politics of unilateralism practiced by the United States and other developed states. Cuba's struggle for development in a world dominated by the United States provides a compelling example to the rest of the Third World of how technological advancement and economic development are inextricably linked to the quest for national sovereignty.

Cuba's recent economic misfortunes have helped the Cuban leadership justify a renewed commitment to an ethic of sacrifice and to the continuation of the struggle to overcome U.S. aggression and imperialism. Castro encountered little difficulty (until the late 1960s) in tapping the tremendous reservoir of sentiment against overt U.S. intervention and in channeling this energy into collective activities designed to support redistributive policies. With the onset of the special period in 1990 (ironically triggered more by the collapse of Soviet support and trade with Eastern Europe than by U.S. aggression), Castro is again capitalizing on stepped-up U.S. sanctions and the pecuniary designs by Cuban exile groups to recolonize Cuba in the "post-Castro" era to justify a resumption of mobilization strategies. The appeal of the call for renewed sacrifice and struggle will depend on Castro's continued success in demonstrating the inseparability of a national identity (as illustrated by his summoning of the spirit of Antonio Maceo and other revolutionary predecessors at the Fourth Party Congress in 1991) and the struggle to achieve an existence free from U.S. domination. But such support is also contingent on whether the special period is perceived as a temporary setback or as a reversal of the occupational and social gains won through extraordinary but ultimately futile efforts.

Castro candidly acknowledged at the Fourth Party Congress, in one of his most frank and sober assessments of the Cuban economic situation, the striking extent of Cuban dependency upon Soviet assistance and trade. Even more astonishing was Castro's admission that extensive multiyear trade agreements with the Soviet Union had been renewed in late 1989 despite increasing uncertainty about the future of communist control. In early 1990 the Soviets began to default on the delivery of oil and other goods imported by Cuba, which had dwindled to a trickle by 1991 (Reed 1992:40–46). There was something disingenuous about Castro's insistence that the sudden change of events in the Soviet Union could not have been anticipated, especially when he claimed credit for warning the Soviets about the potential disaster to socialism lurking in policies of economic liberalization—a direction Castro first initiated with the SDPE and then subsequently repudiated in his policy of rectification, launched in 1986 (Reed 1992:55–56). Nevertheless, the collapse of trade with Eastern Europe and the sharp reduction in Soviet aid may have significant repercussions for the stability of Cuban society and economy as a whole, potentially compromising or weakening the momentum and direction that social change has assumed to this point.

Indeed, more than thirty years of Cuban dependency on trade with the Soviet Union and the former members of the Council of Mutual Economic Assistance detracted from the initiative Cuba could have exercised sooner in achieving technological breakthroughs that would contribute to economic diversification. Cuba was shackled, according to Castro (Reed 1992:42–51, 59), in the 1960s and 1970s to the export of sugar, nickel, and citrus, giving the Soviets tremendous leverage over capital investments and technologies that were likely to serve Cuba's own economic interests.

These trade commitments offered short-term security but encumbered Cuba with the misplaced attempt to increase productivity through the more efficient use of labor rather than the "intensive" application of science and technology (Reed 1992:59). The trade-dictated drive for productivity found expression in heavy-handed policies to promote labor discipline in the early 1970s as well as in more reasonable efforts in the late 1970s and early 1980s to increase worker participation in enterprise planning processes. Cuba also began to export thousands of workers in construction and other trades to Czechoslovakia and other Eastern European countries to offset trade deficits, contributing to considerable shortages in housing and other sectors at home.

The late 1970s marked a significant turning point in Cuban development strategies: Increased synchronization occurred between international assistance programs and investment in health and biomedical technology. Castro's speech to the United Nations in 1979 stressing the "interdependency" of developed and developing countries signaled a new point of departure in Cuba's attempts to put science in the service of human welfare. Castro's farsighted investment in biotechnology not only has increased Cuba's prestige and standing within the United Nations through its medical service missions but also promises to yield a number of medical and agricultural applications that could very well bring about recovery and sustained economic growth. However, this agenda for intensive economic development involves the dedication of enormous resources to the health sector, continually enlarging the role that scientists, physicians, and other professionals play in determining the direction of social development. Cuban citizens have become increasingly entangled in a web of social services and health interventions of questionable necessity that intrude on the domain of autonomy, privacy, and rights.

The Sequence of Social Transformation

The Cuban revolution unleashed a complex and contradictory set of forces that coalesced in a series of strategic struggles to define the methods of governance by which to achieve a just social order. The distinctiveness of the Cuban revolution, which sets it apart from other socialist regimes, is that it embodies more than an attempt to overcome the forces of legal domination and economic exploitation characteristic of capitalist states. It constitutes an effort to reorganize the biological and psychological factors that limit one's capacity to be productive under stress and to contribute selflessly to the welfare of a collectivity without an expectation of personal reward. There is a recognizable emphasis on virtue in this scheme of self-transformation, but it goes beyond considerations of character. The ethic of sacrifice, as Castro and Guevara understood it, necessitated the redefinition of the conditions of subjectivity. Individuality is no longer defined solely by a set of formal and inviolable rights and interests; rather, it is distinguished by one's attitude toward family, work, and community life and by one's capacity to undergo discipline and be trained to live up to expectations imposed by conscience and standards of well-being.

The series of strategic struggles documented in the foregoing chapters that Cuba has undergone during the process of social reconstruction approximates in certain ways the sequence that, Foucault contends, brought about the transformation of premodern regimes based on sovereignty and rights into modern (or perhaps postmodern) regimes based on bureaucratic rationality and disciplinary techniques of normalization. There has been a systematic attempt in Cuba to replace the Western juridical conception of human dignity based on autonomy, privacy, and self-interest with one predicated on conscience, social conduct, and well-being. The Cuban leadership has sought the assistance of professional experts in finding scientific equivalents for these human values that can serve as norms to guide individual development and group behavior.

However, the processes of social development in Cuba also show evidence of diverging from the sequel predicted by Foucault. A regime dedicated to reliance on interdisciplinary scientific research in social problem solving coexists uneasily alongside an anachronistic party regime governed by patronage and riddled with corruption. The Cuban leadership precariously straddles styles of governance characteristic of different eras. The regime of patronage requires an abiding and uncritical loyalty to a charismatic patriarch. In contrast, the regime of normalization requires an unequivocal dedication to scientific truth, not obeisance to a sovereign. The virtue of sacrifice finds few converts, and much cynicism and resistance, in a system unable to reconcile the disparity between a reward system based on loyalty and one built on knowledge and discipline. By this reckoning, Cuba has not yet transcended the cycle of reform and retrenchment that has undermined the consummation of progressive policies for social and political transformation undertaken by other developed or developing nations. Nevertheless, the Cuban leadership is making a concerted effort to change the attitudes, habits, routines, and behavior that block the complete transition from tradition-bound societies to polities governed by equality, justice, and human dignity.

The distinctiveness of Cuban social development as well as its current dilemmas can best be illustrated by drawing together the strands of evidence presented in the previous chapters. The Cuban experiment in popular justice was undertaken precisely to loosen the grip that an overly formalistic and rigid prerevolutionary legal system had exercised in sustaining vast inequities in the distribution of wealth and public services.

Cuban citizens were encouraged to temper judgment of their peers with compassion and sensitivity to the difficulties inherent in the effort to learn behavior appropriate to the norms governing conduct in a socialist state. Law was used as a pedagogical instrument to promote increased awareness of the principles of socialist distribution during a period of severe shortages and rationing. Significantly, the CDRs were expected to play essential but conflicting roles in distributing scarce goods and administering justice. This compromised the rule of law and created an opening for the organization and deployment of illegalities.

As indispensable as the CDRs were in enabling the Cuban leadership to consolidate its control in the early years of the revolution, they were ill-equipped to bring about a social system based on universal norms of social judgment. Weak external controls (i.e., party supervision) and a diffuse, heterogeneous membership with divergent interests and goals proved to be serious constraints to the fulfillment of the CDR mandate to promote participation based on a common conception of virtuous conduct and social justice. Decisions of the People's Courts involved judgments reflecting parochial values and interests and served in many instances to reinforce guilt or resentment rather than change the status quo. To be sure, the CDRs generated substantial participation in local projects involving direct benefits to community residents. However, they were unable to sustain enthusiasm and effectively coordinate mobilization on a larger, national-interest-based scale, such as that required in the 1970 sugar harvest, without encountering substantial resistance in the form of soaring absenteeism and withdrawal of support. Increasingly robbed of a constituency to serve, the CDRs lost control over their mission and role and now are confined largely to a surveillance and crime-prevention function.

The focus in the 1970s shifted from participation to productivity and advancement. The Cuban leadership sought ways to increase economic growth through the use of moral incentives. However, a system of emulation by itself proved to be incapable of significantly altering workers' motives and attitudes. Economic planners failed to redesign the processes of work so that labor was intrinsically satisfying rather than instrumental to material reward or some other self-interested aim. Moreover, low productivity and absenteeism appeared to persist because of widespread management collusion and corruption. Castro sought methods that would dissolve these worker-employer networks and increase his capacity to determine the allocation and distribution of scarce resources. The Cuban authorities initially relied on a juridical and punitive approach, which ironically contributed to increased union protection of workers' rights.

Among the factors contributing to political decentralization in the mid-1970s and increased worker participation in enterprise planning was the realization that the PCC could not effectively provide political leadership and control the day-to-day administration of the national economy. The Escalante microfaction demonstrated that the attempt to combine policymaking and administration was a recipe for role conflict and corruption. The SDPE and the OPP provided complementary tools to enable the PCC to divest itself of direct responsibility for allocative decisions by making enterprises and service providers partially accountable to workers, their union representatives, and local governments. These strategies to institutionalize new approaches to production and governance have had contrasting and mixed results.

Under the SDPE, workers and their union representatives acquired control over grievance processes and made a concerted effort to challenge management prerogatives on a variety of issues impinging on workers' rights, including hiring, promotion, transfer, compensation, and discipline for infractions. The FMC was particularly successful in increasing women's participation in the work force by attacking arbitrary forms of discrimination and barriers to employment. But only limited progress was made by workers to acquire more influence in the planning process.

In contrast, many enterprise managers appeared to have abused their newly acquired freedom under the SDPE to set production priorities by misallocating or diverting resources and/or collaborating with free farmers' markets in a great variety of illegal transactions to enrich themselves and their associates. Managers also stubbornly resisted worker attempts to undermine their discretion by refusing to implement worker council decisions, no doubt contributing to the dramatic increase in judicial appeals in the late 1970s and early 1980s.

These contrasting consequences of decentralization raise a perplexing question: Why did the Cuban leadership elect, with its policy of rectification in the mid-1980s, not only to reassert greater central control over enterprise production but also to seemingly weaken, if not reverse, the trend toward a union-led democratization process? It is conceivable that had the CTC been allowed to vigorously pursue workers' rights issues, management abuses and corruption could have been brought under closer scrutiny and control without eliminating decentralized planning. Moreover, the national arbitration unit certainly appeared to be making headway in the attempt to challenge and correct questionable uses of enterprise resources.

Not choosing these alternative options cannot be explained solely in terms of economic rationality or political logic. The increased freedom and discretion enterprise managers enjoyed under the SDPE, Castro believed, contributed to a mercantilist attitude that threatened to undermine the moral foundations of socialism. Indeed, the logic of economic growth was not sufficient to justify the diversion of energy and resources into goods and services of dubious social value. This encouraged consumption, not investment, and robbed the regime of its exclusive authority to control the system of reward based on one's contribution to the common good.

The trend toward increased worker participation and workers' rights presents a more troublesome dilemma. Despite his misgivings about the CTC leadership throughout the 1960s, Castro realized that union support was essential to economic growth and regime support. He also learned that workers had as much a stake in the planning and production processes as they do in the output. Production norms by themselves did little to stimulate increased productivity when the worker was treated unfairly or arbitrarily. Moreover, union representation of worker grievances showed the potential of becoming an effective tool for dismantling the cadre-dominated "good old boy" network that was blocking, in many instances, the most effective use of human resources.

So why did the Cuban leadership choose to strengthen management's power to discipline workers rather than support more vigorous enforcement of laws protecting workers' rights? Four factors appear salient. First, patronage continues to serve as the primary conduit for advancement to middle- and higher-level jobs in Cuba. Changing this facet of power threatens the leadership's capacity to demand loyalty and the observance of prescribed conduct in exchange for recognition and advancement. Second, the CTC serves as an umbrella organization representing diverse and highly specialized occupations. However, union support for specialization is inconsistent with leadership demands (and psychological evidence) that specific work tasks not be monopolized by any one group and that there be flexibility, rather than rigidity, among participants in the labor force.

Third, the protection of rights involves a legalistic and potentially divisive juridical approach to solving Cuba's social problems. Rights imply that there are specific and sometimes competing interests involved in a policy issue. But the strength of the Cuban revolution, as Castro conceives it, rests on unity and a universal conception of human dignity and the common good. The weaknesses of the OPP illustrate well how easily a system designed to facilitate representation and accountability, yet limit conflict and divisiveness, can get swallowed up by legal formalism, parochialism, and corruption.

Castro's enormous appeal rests in part on his ability to enunciate clearly defined national goals and objectives and to provide leadership toward their attainment. However, the OPP is not organized to enable delegates to participate in the formulation of national priorities, nor does it enable delegates to collect information sufficient for them to take a broader perspective on the kinds of problems facing each locality. It should not be surprising, therefore, to find that disenchantment with the OPP is widespread because delegates are unable to influence or change the intermediate cadre-dominated structures through which local concerns must pass in order to get translated into national policy. Yet there are signs (discussed later) that cadre strength is weakening at intermediate levels as Castro seeks to streamline and redirect PCC activity toward the localities.

Finally, Castro maintains a long-standing conviction (reinforced by the failure of popular justice) that the problems confronting social development in Cuba will and can be solved only by science, not by law. In the early 1970s Vilma Espín farsightedly launched a study of child growth that signaled a new point of departure in the processes of social development. Social policies would no longer be dictated solely by intuition or emulation but would be guided by experimental studies and social research. The focus of this research has been to discover the biological and psychological factors that shape individual conduct, including the capacity to be productive and contribute selflessly to societal welfare. Psychologists and other social scientists are trying to understand how to overcome factors that promote acceptance or increase resistance to change in living habits, family roles, child-rearing practices, work structures, professional aspirations, and so forth. Perhaps the most significant obstacle to change is the persistence of patrimonialism, clientism, and provincialism, which defy the consistent application of objective criteria to guide, appraise, and reward appropriate conduct. This conduct contributes to uncertainty and dissonance.

As illustrated in previous chapters, the rapid pace of change in the 1960s contributed to social exhaustion by the end of the decade. Family life was undergoing a breakdown, and delinquency took on major proportions. New strategies were needed to cope with these problems. The result has been a discernible trend toward the articulation and adoption of scientific norms to regulate human conduct. Cuban social policymakers have also come to the belated recognition that there is probably no substitute for the love, affection, guidance, and role models that parents provide their children and that these factors are just as important (if not more so) as peer group influences in contributing to normal development. Cuban psychologists have determined that attitudes and habits are shaped in early childhood by the quality and effectiveness of communication processes that are difficult to change at a later age. The FMC is now shifting attention toward family structure and may very well strike an effective balance between implementing necessary changes in the traditional sexual division of labor and sustaining attitudes supportive of mutual respect and cooperation in child-rearing and work. The Cuban response to the problems of gender stereotypes and child development contrasts sharply to Chinese strategies of population control, described in Chapter 4, which have cynically exploited traditional family hierarchies and attitudes to institute market-oriented modernization schemes.

However, what distinguishes Cuban society from the disciplinary society of normalization described by Foucault is the conscious attempt to use scientific knowledge to tease out or evoke the heroic virtues and to strengthen the capacity for resistance and self-transformation that Castro believes lies latent in every human being. Cuban strategies for social development, unlike those methods Foucault (1979) describes in disciplinary regimes, have not been derived from experimentation in sites where individuals are isolated and clinically differentiated from one another and from agents of intervention in prisons, asylums, or hospitals. Instead, social knowledge comes from studies of how persons (i.e., agents of intervention and recipients) *interact* in group processes involving mutual problem solving within the larger environment in which they are situated. This mode of experimentation has been characteristic of the evolving polyclinic and family doctor health programs as well as of the attempts to develop alternative work structures and mechanisms for local governance.

Civic Virtue and the Dilemma of Rights

The study of factors affecting attitudes and behavior in groups shows promise in contributing important insights about the conditions that favor the development of leadership and selflessness, higher thresholds of resistance to stress, and increased susceptibility to moral appeals and sacrifice. But it is unlikely that men and women who embody these virtues and capacities will not also be resourceful and seek the discretion and independent judgment necessary to forge new solutions to Cuba's most pressing economic and social problems. As Connolly (1987:114), an astute theorist of the dilemmas facing democracy in modernity, observes, the collectivist ideal of a legitimate state requires civic virtue to bear more weight than it can support in achieving social unity because that ideal presupposes, incorrectly, too close a fit between the characteristics of a well ordered society and those of an integrated individual. Connolly (1987:114–15) contends that "an order with slack can sustain itself well without the need to organize the self so completely into a creature of virtue. For the more an order needs virtue, the more it eventually authorizes the extension of disciplinary strategies to secure it. . . . Slack at once reduces the space virtue must cover and enhances the prospects for civic virtue within the space appropriate to it."

If the ideals and standards of a social order are too demanding and unattainable, cynicism rapidly fills the space vacated by virtue, and evasion becomes an acceptable mode of adaptation. But contrary to Huntington's (1981) thesis about modernization (see the Introduction), hypocrisy and cynicism do not inevitably result in a failure of will, loss of confidence, and retrenchment. The Polish revolt against communist hypocrisy demonstrated that resentment can be converted into cooperation and trust within and among disparate groups and that optimism can be sustained by pursuing a collective purpose and a common identity. Similarly, Cuba's internationalist strategy for world development generates national pride, instead of envy, and continues to inspire the search by the United Nations to find collective solutions to the world's most pressing human and environmental problems.

Some observers have applauded the recent demise of communism in Eastern Europe and the Soviet Union because they expect to see soon the revival of civil society and with it a renewal of individual rights, which they claim were extinguished under socialism and communism (see Rau 1991). However, I believe that it is mistaken and misleading to contend that socialist and capitalist states can be distinguished merely by the presence or absence of civil society. The term *civil society* cannot be defined without oversimplification, as Rau (1991:4–5) does, as that sphere of social life involving the "spontaneous and voluntary exchange" of resources, services, or other goods. Western governments and multinational corporations are heavily engaged in the planned (rather than the spontaneous) investment and use (or squandering) of scarce resources, and there is scarcely a realm of private transactions that is not subject to state regulation or judicial intervention. (For critiques of the Western, liberal conception of civil society, see Gray 1991; Arato 1991.)

Moreover, controversy over discrimination, abortion, school prayer, and many other social issues pertaining to individual attitudes and choice in Western nations has obscured the boundary between public and private spheres of behavior. Consequently, it would be more accurate to think of civil society in terms of a continuum of potentially free activities and relationships subject to some degree of relative constraint. The pervasive existence of informal networks in Cuba and other socialist states indicates that interactions of every kind occur without government sanction and that these networks set limits to the feasible reach of state control.

It also is misleading to say (or imply, as does Rau 1991) that since socialist regimes do not acknowledge or protect the Western juridical conception of individual rights, they are incapable of becoming democratic societies. The Cuban experience suggests, however, that rights do not exist apart from the social roles and institutional norms that regulate individual behavior. Rights are not transcendental but circumstantial; they confer a status on the individual by virtue of the role performed and the relationships entered into with other persons in social groups and institutions. Law simply formalizes the status and routinizes the expected conduct of individuals, who become involved in relationships by virtue of their roles, such as that between husband and wife, parents and children, and employer and employee. The real issue at stake is whether the norms regulating conduct encourage individual judgment and promote equality and solidarity rather than conformity, suspicion, resentment, and intolerance.

The challenge that Cuban authorities face, then, is to create sufficient slack in the social order (i.e., loosening role requirements and routines) for experimentation that provides people with the instrumentalities (i.e., knowledge and techniques) and freedom necessary to forge new solutions to problems that none can escape alone. Biotechnology shows great promise in helping Cuba overcome imprisonment in a sugar monoculture, while advances in biomedicine may contribute significantly to the well-being of the Cuban population. But these life sciences also threaten to substitute the laboratory for natural sites of social experimentation and rob Cuban workers of the opportunity to choose the techniques that will enable Cuba to cross the frontier between scarcity/rationing and abundance/diversity.

Moreover, a standard of well-being does not by itself provide unambiguous, intersubjective criteria to measure differences in welfare, enrichment, and personal satisfaction yielded by improvements in health compared to the opportunities or advances affecting other realms of human experience (Elster 1991; Kahneman and Varey 1991). Nor can the legitimacy of a regime be based solely on its capability to provide for the general welfare or common good without reducing governance to a crude utilitarianism indifferent to individual interests.

Cuba must somehow find a way to enable citizens to develop autonomous personalities, acquire and defend interests, and maintain loyalties through primary group attachments and affiliations that contribute to societal diversity without undermining mechanisms for strong, progressive leadership dedicated to a common national purpose. A conception of rights based on the shared interests of specific occupational groups (i.e., resources allocated for training, specializations available, and working conditions) and the collective contribution they make to societal well-being (measured by some weighted scale of the value of goods and services) could be articulated that is consistent with the common good. For example, workers' rights policies patterned after laws such as the Family Code or existing regulations protecting women's rights could be established. Standards governing discretionary professional judgments could be adopted that protect the integrity and autonomy of the individual without sacrificing the general welfare.

Issue Networks and Policy Implementation

The different strategies employed to bring about social development in Cuba have also contributed to changes in the structures or circuits through which influence and knowledge are routed and brought to bear in national policies affecting economic growth and societal well-being. Party cadres no longer dominate the implementation of national policies; they now share this intermediary role with professionals, who compete for influence in policymaking processes. This situation did not occur suddenly. It emerged as a result of changes in the configuration and strength of network ties forged by leaders of mass organizations and professionals, altering the methods and pathways through which knowledge and influence are translated into political action. Network analysis provides some useful tools by which to gain insights about the relationship between processes of social development and changes in the structure of power in Cuba.

Social systems governed by centralized political authorities depend strongly on effective lines of communication and the exchange of information among leaders, intermediaries, and recipients. Several properties of networks involving the circulation, exchange, dissemination, and retrieval of information and resources are pertinent to our analysis (Knoke 1990). Networks can be differentiated by the pattern of relationships exhibited among members of subgroups. For example, subgroups that are characterized by strong mutual social ties or economic interests, such as members of the PCC, and that are in frequent and direct contact and interaction and receive information from multiple sources are likely to occupy positions of centrality in the political system. In contrast, access to authorities and policymaking processes by subgroup members at the periphery of these circles is determined by their capacity to occupy positions that are structurally equivalent—that is, positions that provide comparable opportunities to compete for the attention or influence of decisionmakers through third-party intermediaries. For example, an individual who coordinates the CDRs has roughly the same access to party intermediaries or other proximate officials as does the individual who coordinates a polyclinic team in that same sector.

The paths that connect central and peripheral subgroups vary in terms of distance and reachability. Distance is measured by the number and sequence of intervening links required to connect the sender and the receiver of messages. Reachability refers to the strength of the connections between individuals. For example, individuals are strongly connected in a network if the ties between subgroups are bidirectional or reciprocal. A social system that relies on hierarchy and unidirectional communication through the chain of command may be efficient, but it limits or discourages the feedback essential to effective implementation and adjustment.

Subgroups on the periphery tend to be weakly connected to central decisionmakers. This characteristic enables intermediaries to work at the margins between groups, brokering influence and information in ways that determine how more remote elements will be integrated into the larger social system. Thus, intermediaries may strongly influence how information is circulated and how innovations are diffused within society as a whole. Leaders of mass organizations or professionals who also serve as incumbents in other official roles may be more successful in performing this integrative function by virtue of possessing more extensive contacts and resources that can be mobilized to implement a program.

A final element used to differentiate networks according to relative influence and power is prominence. This is defined by the visibility an individual or a subgroup has in the political system through proximity to central leaders and by the number of direct and indirect ties to other influential persons or groups. One avenue to prominence in Cuba is the prestige conferred by party membership, which provides opportunities for advancement to positions of influence in exchange for dedication, loyalty, and support. Charisma and strong leadership skills constitute another resource that can be used to acquire positions of authority (as in the case of Castro and Guevara) and/or that can be channeled into modes of resistance and opposition (as illustrated by the Escalante and Ochoa affairs). Another route is the acquisition of knowledge and expertise and the persuasive application of techniques to solve pressing social or scientific problems. Individuals who possess expertise are likely to attract the attention or ire of central decisionmakers by attaining positions that enable them to determine the flow of information and coordinate the use of resources involved in the implementation and evaluation of policies.

Let us return to the evidence presented in this book to identify how issue networks have changed over time. The experiment in popular justice in the 1960s constituted a significant test of the capacity of the regime to achieve rapid social change by relying primarily on the CDRs and other mass organizations to implement this strategy of mobilization. The CDR leadership, however, was encumbered with conflicting roles that made it difficult, even under ideal conditions, to keep responsibilities for distribution separate from the administration of justice. The Escalante faction skillfully exploited the tenuous and weak mechanisms of supervision and control established by party cadres by developing extensive networks of exchange among the CDR ranks. The People's Courts were set up separately and completely outside the existing judicial system, little effort was made to gain support from legal professionals, and no mechanism existed to bring about the consistent and comprehensive diffusion and evaluation of the merits and drawbacks of this program. These weaknesses of coordination and integration contributed decisively to the termination of this innovation and to a considerable contraction of CDR functions and political influence.

This approach was followed by the attempt to give professional specialists and technicians the responsibility for coordinating programs and services to specially targeted areas and groups, such as those services provided by physicians in area polyclinics and medicine in the community program. Physicians were expected to cooperate with one another and with members of mass organizations in establishing a health profile of the community so that they could meet the specific needs of chronic patients while also drawing up a plan to prevent these and other health problems from recurring. An attempt was made to ensure a uniform distribution of polyclinic staff, and teamwork was emphasized in the delivery of services.

However, many of the difficulties and deficiencies of this approach stemmed from the configuration of the preexisting network of professional relationships. For example, polyclinic staff remained dependent on specialist consultation with hospital staff and on the use of its resources. In-house staff collaboration in patient treatment occurred infrequently and usually only involved physicians in closely allied fields. Staff physicians also failed in most instances to enlist mass organizations in a cooperative effort in case finding and rarely completed or updated surveys of the health conditions of their sectors. Consequently, public health officials received little worthwhile feedback in planning for the health needs of the population to anticipate threats to public health.

The reluctance or unwillingness of polyclinic physicians to fulfill these various tasks effectively as intermediaries in the health system was related to the structure of prestige and advancement. Prestige was defined by effectiveness in curative, rather than preventive, health, and advancement was ultimately contingent on further specialization through paths of training and experience dictated by leaders in the profession. These pathways to success were unlikely to change, as Castro discovered through subsequent evaluations, without a thoroughgoing reform of the medical profession.

Two varieties of specialist intervention were also used in the treatment and rehabilitation of delinquent youth. In the mid-1960s the military collaborated with the FMC, the CTC, and other groups in operating special training and reeducation programs for delinquent youth on the Isle of Pines, in Matanzas, and in other provinces. These programs were organized to provide structured and disciplined living experience and apprenticeship training under the tutelage of strong, charismatic role models. Vilma Espín (1991:47) indicated that this approach, which she initiated (and which is now being revived in the Blas Roca contingents), aroused opposition from the labor movement and intruded on the domain of the CDRs and the professionals, both of whom organized local delinquency prevention committees in the 1970s and 1980s. However, by the late 1980s officials and professionals in the Ministry of the Interior had created new legislation that put delinquency programs under national jurisdiction to ensure more consistency and effectiveness in diagnostic and treatment modalities.

Only after an extended period of institutionalization and experimentation, including the strengthening of the field of psychology and the production of social research, was it possible to remedy the defects of the populist (i.e., courts and juvenile justice) and specialist issue networks. The evaluation of the Matanzas experiment in health care, and subsequent work and mental-health-related programs, offered psychologists a chance to demonstrate the significant contribution that their knowledge and techniques could make in overcoming obstacles to social and professional development. Their studies convinced Castro that a body of experimental knowledge about human behavior could be applied to obtain conduct thoroughly consistent with the principles and objectives he and Guevara had articulated to form the new person in socialism. Psychologists have reaped the benefits of this success by increasing their professional prestige. They have acquired greater influence in social policy by attempting to lead the health system toward the fulfillment of a mandate for societal well-being.

In addition, Castro realized the usefulness of evaluations in providing feedback for fine-tuning policy as well as in increasing his leverage in overcoming rigidities in the medical profession that blocked the development of preventive health care. Castro's demand for coordination in problem solving has led to the creation of interdisciplinary networks entailing cooperation among researchers and scientists in the production and application of techniques of social knowledge. Vilma Espín continues to provide leadership in establishing temporary task forces and commissions that provide flexibility and independence from ministry bureaucracy and interference.

Another mode of policymaking that surfaced in the 1970s, which proved to be controversial, was the creation of what I call special-interest networks. Two examples of this kind of issue network described in Chapter 3 were the women's front created within the CTC in the early 1970s and the commission handling workers' grievances through workers' councils when that authority was lodged in the CTC from 1977 through 1980. The women's front was created to increase female participation in the work force and combat discrimination. These objectives were connected to the overall goals of attaining equality of the sexes in families and providing equal opportunities for women to participate in and attain leadership positions in managerial and political institutions.

The most significant outcome of these continuing efforts has been the creation of opportunities for women to attain positions structurally equivalent in authority and responsibility to men. For example, women constitute more than 50 percent of the candidates recruited for the family doctor program, more than 56 percent of all top-level technicians, and a significant percentage of psychologists. Moreover, women are making substantial inroads in the biological sciences, conducting research that will determine Cuba's future. Significantly, women who participate in these fields and programs acquire potentially more direct ties to Castro by virtue of his intimate involvement in overseeing these endeavors. However, resistance among enterprise and work-center managers remains strong, most likely because affirmative action undermines the practice of *sociolismo* and party patronage.

CTC control over grievance processes provided workers an opportunity to challenge the almost unlimited prerogatives of managers to exercise arbitrary, prejudicial, and sometimes vindictive control over workers' careers. Workers filed grievances and appeals involving conflicts in domains heretofore considered sacrosanct, such as hiring, promotion, and transfer for disciplinary reasons. The momentum produced by the rising tide of these legal challenges spilled over into the National Assembly, which initiated a national (but never completed) survey to determine whether specific management abuses fit some recurring nationwide pattern. Again, the stakes were too high for the regime to let that study go forward. I believe that the real threat posed by this investigation was not so much the potential for compromising the integrity of the PCC as the political repercussions of the incipient alliance emerging between the CTC and delegates of the National Assembly to address these issues. For unlike the women's equality issue, advanced carefully and judiciously by a trusted member of the inner circle, Vilma Espín, the movement for workers' rights threatened to quickly slip out of the grasp and control of the Cuban leadership. So far, the regime has not been successful in finding an adequate solution to the problem of workers' rights, which promises to grow more troublesome.

What are the implications of these changes in the configuration of issue networks for understanding the structure of power and policymaking in Cuba? The foregoing analysis supports three general observations. First, Castro is increasingly centralizing and consolidating his control over social and science policies. The family doctor program perhaps epitomizes his leadership style. Castro created the program, made it a priority in the health system, developed guidelines for recruitment, effectuated changes in existing institutions to accommodate the program, created direct lines of accountability of staff to himself, and subjected every aspect of the program to his continual review and intervention. This sequence of involvement was repeated in the creation of the People's Councils in 1990.

The Blas Roca contingents represent an interesting attempt to restore, under different guises, the apprenticeship concept that Vilma Espín first championed in the late 1960s. The program constitutes Castro's vision for the future structure of work and is significant enough to merit representation on the Politburo by its director, Palmero Hernández. Finally, Castro created a small advisory group of scientists to obtain guidance on priorities and advise him on the research conducted at the Center for Biotechnology and Genetic Engineering. Significantly, this group works completely outside of the control of the Cuban Academy of Sciences and the party apparatus.

Second, the roles of party cadres and professionals as intermediaries in policymaking and implementation have changed. Clearly, in the early years of the revolution party cadres were the gatekeepers: They exercised nearly exclusive control over the processes of recognition and advancement. However, because of their small numbers, cadres had to rely on an extensive network of lower-level functionaries in mass organizations, such as the CDRs and the CTC, to extend their span of control. This had the unfortunate consequence of tolerating ineptitude and inconsistency and breeding corruption and indifference. The changes made in the PCC with the introduction of the OPP acknowledged that the party had overextended itself and that the PCC would divest itself of an operational role. This was a fateful decision, for it cleared the way for the introduction of the expertise that was so desperately needed to address social problems. This situation has not eliminated patronage, but it has contained patronage within a smaller domain than it once occupied. Professionals have quietly slipped into and filled these gaps in the cadres' terrain and are attempting to substitute a new ethic based, not on cronyism and quid pro quo, but on expertise and discipline through teamwork and coordination.

Third, despite the enormous resources and effort that Castro and the Cuban leadership are putting into the formation of interdisciplinary networks for the application of social and scientific knowledge, social policies continue to reflect the sometimes inconsistent and conflicting interests of different groups in Cuban society. A forum is available in the National Assembly, among other institutions, to allow these conflicts to be aired, and proposals have been made to give delegates a more significant role in accumulating and evaluating information bearing on Cuban social policies. Although the outcome of these and other resolutions made at the Fourth Party Congress remains uncertain, the long-term survival of the Cuban revolution will depend on whether its leaders choose to deploy knowledge to strengthen systems of social constraint and dependency or to expand the role of its citizens and nonparty members in governance so that Cuba may break free from the cycle of corruption, reform, and retrenchment that has contributed to the recent downfall of so many other one-party socialist states.

References

Almond, G.A., ed. 1989. *The Civic Culture Revisited*. Newbury Park, Calif.: Sage.

Almond, G.A., and S. Verba. 1965. *The Civic Culture: Political Attitudes and Democracy in Five Nations*. Boston: Little, Brown.

Alvaréz Díaz, J. et al. 1963. *Labor Conditions in Communist Cuba*. Miami: University of Miami Press.

Alzugaray Treto, C. 1991. "Problems of National Security in the Cuban-U.S. Historic Breach." In *U.S.-Cuban Relations in the 1990s*, ed. J. Domínguez and R. Hernández. Boulder, Colo.: Westview.

Americas Watch. 1984. *Critique: Review of the Department of State's Country Reports on Human Rights Practices for 1983*. New York: Americas Watch.

Amnesty International. 1987. *Political Imprisonment in Cuba*. Washington, D.C.: Cuban American Foundation.

Arato, A. 1991. "Revolution, Civil Society, and Democracy." In *The Reemergence of Civil Society in Eastern Europe and the Soviet Union*, ed. Z. Rau. Boulder, Colo.: Westview.

Ardila, R. 1982. "Psicología y Terapia del Comportamiento." *Revista del Hospital Psiquiátrico de la Habana* 23:507–22.

Arnove, R., and H. Graff, eds. 1987. *National Literacy Campaigns: Historical and Comparative Perspectives*. New York: Plenum.

Avila Naún, V. et al. 1986. "La Relación Medico-Paciente Valorada por el Enfermo." *Boletín de Psicología* 9(3):129–48.

Azicri, M. 1979a. "The Institutionalization of the Cuban Revolution: A Review of the Literature." *Cuban Studies* 9(2):63–90.

———. 1979b. "Women's Development Through Revolutionary Mobilization: A Study of the Federation of Cuban Women." *International Journal of Women's Studies* 2(2):27–50.

———. 1980a. "Crime and Law Under Socialism: The 1979 Cuban Penal Code." *Review of Socialist Law* 6(1):5–20.

———. 1980b. "The Cuban Family Code: Some Observations on Its Innovations and Continuities." *Review of Socialist Law* 6(2):183–91.

———. 1980c. "An Introduction to Cuban Socialist Law." *Review of Socialist Law* 6(2):153–63.

———. 1981. "Crime, Penal Law, and the Cuban Revolutionary Process." *Crime and Social Justice* 2:51–79.

———. 1985. "Socialist Legality and Practice: The Cuban Experience." In *Cuba: Twenty-Five Years of Revolution, 1959–1984*. New York: Praeger.

————. 1988. *Cuba: Politics, Economics and Society.* London: Pinter.

Baloyra, E. 1987. "Political Control and Cuban Youth." Paper presented at the roundtable conference Youth in Cuba Today: The Next Generation, sponsored by Radio Martí, Washington, D.C., November 6.

Baum, L. 1981. "Comparing the Implementation of Legislative and Judicial Policies." In *Effective Policy Implementation,* ed. P. Sabatier and D. Mazmanian. Lexington, Mass.: D.C. Heath.

Beardsley, T. 1986. "Cuban Biotechnology: Progress Despite Isolation." *Nature* 320 (March 6):2.

Beckwith, J. 1985. "Cuba Report: Science and Society Are Inseparable." *Science for the People* (September-October):20–24.

Benglesdorf, C. 1988a. "Cubanology and Crises: The Mainstream Looks at Institutionalization in Cuban Political Economy." In *Cuban Political Economy,* ed. A. Zimbalist. Boulder, Colo.: Westview.

————. 1988b. "On the Problem of Studying Women in Cuba." In *Cuban Political Economy,* ed. A. Zimbalist. Boulder, Colo.: Westview.

————. 1990. "The Matter of Democracy in Cuba: Snapshots of Three Moments." In *Transformation and Struggle: Cuba Faces the 1990s,* ed. S. Halebsky and J.M. Kirk. New York: Praeger.

Bergenn, V., T.C. Dalton, and L.P. Lipsitt. 1992. "Myrtle B. McGraw: A Growth Scientist." *Developmental Psychology* 28(3):381–95.

Berman, H., and N.R. Whiting. 1980. "Impressions of Cuban Law." *American Journal of Comparative Law* 28(3):475–86.

Berman, J. 1969. "The Cuban Popular Tribunals." *Columbia Law Review* 69:1317–54.

Bernal, G. 1985. "A History of Psychology in Cuba." *Journal of Community Psychology* 13(2):222–35.

Bernal, G., and E. Isern. 1986. "La Terapia Familar y la Ideología." *Revista Cubana de Psicología* 3(2):15–20.

Betto, F. 1987. *Fidel and Religion.* New York: Simon and Schuster.

Bohr, D.F. 1979. "President-Elect's Tour: Changes in Cuba." *The Physiologist* 22:9–11.

Boletín de Psicología. 1982. "Sección Estudiantil: Relación Médico-Paciente: Su Utilización por Estudiantes de Medicina." *Boletín de Psicología* 5(1):95–103.

Bonachea, R.L., and M. San Martin. 1974. *The Cuban Insurrection, 1952–1959.* New Brunswick, N.J.: Transaction.

Brady, J.P. 1982. *Justice and Politics in People's China: Legal Order or Continuing Revolution?* New York: Academic.

————. 1983. "Crime, Justice, and Community in Socialist Cuba." *International Annals of Criminology* 20(1–2):5–32.

Brown, A., and J. Gray, eds. 1977. *Political Culture and Political Change in Communist States.* New York: Holms Meier.

Burt, R.S., and M. Minor. 1983. *Applied Network Analysis.* Beverly Hills, Calif.: Sage.

Butterworth, D. 1974. "Grassroots Political Organization in Cuba: A Case for Committees for the Defense of the Revolution." In *Latin American Urban Research,* ed. W. Cornelius and F. Trueblood. Beverly Hills, Calif.: Sage.

Calviño, M. 1983. "Experimental-Diagnostic Study of the Semantic Structure of Consciousness." *Revista del Hospital Psiquiátrico de la Habana* 23:59–74.

Camayd-Freixas, Y. 1985a. "Psychiatric Social Epidemiology in Cuba: Contextual Considerations." *Journal of Community Psychology* 13(2):162–72.

———. 1985b. "Psychiatric Social Epidemiology in Cuba II." *Journal of Community Psychology* 13(2):179–93.

Camayd-Freixas, Y., and M. Uriate. 1980. "The Organization of Mental Health Services in Cuba." *Hispanic Journal of Behavioral Sciences* 2(4):337–54.

Campos-Outcalt, D.C., and D.E. Janoff. 1980. "Health Care in Modern Cuba." *Western Journal of Medicine* 132:265–71.

Cardoso, F., and E. Falleto. 1979. *Dependency and Development in Latin America.* Berkeley and Los Angeles: University of California Press.

Carrobello, C. et al. 1990. "Magazine Poll: What Do People Think of Their Power?" *Bohemia* (July 6):5–9.

Casal, L. 1975. "On Popular Power: The Organization of the Cuban State During a Period of Transition." *Latin American Perspectives* 2(4):78–88.

Castellanos, I. 1953. "The Evolution of Criminology in Cuba, 1933–1951." *Journal of Criminal Law and Criminology* 24:218–29.

Castellanos Simons, B., and A.G. Hernández. 1987. "La Esfera Motivacional de la Personalidad y la Sexualidad." *Boletín de Psicología* 10(2):17–29.

Castro, F. 1968. "Year of Solidarity." Speech made at the May Day Celebration Anniversary, Plaza de la Revolución, May 1, 1966. In *Major Speeches.* London: Layston.

———. 1975. *Education in Revolution.* Havana: Instituto del Libro.

———. 1976. "Discurso en el Quince Aniversario de la Fundación del Ministerio del Interior." *Bohemia* (June 11):53–54.

———. 1981. "Speech given to the Thirty-fourth Session of the United Nations General Assembly." October 12, 1979. In *Fidel Castro's Speeches: Cuba's Internationalist Foriegn Policy, 1975–1980,* ed. M. Taber. New York: Pathfinder.

———. 1983a. *The World Economic and Social Crisis.* Havana: Council of State.

———. 1983b. "Against Bureaucracy and Sectarianism." March 26, 1962. In *Fidel Castro's Speeches, Vol. II: Our Power Is That of the Working People,* ed. M. Taber. New York: Pathfinder.

———.1983c. "1970 Self-Criticism: Speech to the Federation of Cuban Women." August 23, 1970. In *Fidel Castro's Speeches, Vol. II: Our Power Is That of the Working People,* ed. M. Taber. New York: Pathfinder.

———. 1983d. "The Need for a Democratic Labor Movement." September 2–3, 1970. In *Fidel Castro's Speeches, Vol. II: Our Power Is That of the Working People,* ed. M. Taber. New York: Pathfinder.

———. 1983e. "The Democratization of the Revolutionary Process." September 28, 1970. In *Fidel Castro's Speeches, Vol. II: Our Power Is That of the Working People,* ed. M. Taber. New York: Pathfinder.

———. 1983f. "The Establishment of People's Power." July 26, 1974. In *Fidel Castro's Speeches, Vol. II: Our Power Is That of the Working People,* ed. M. Taber. New York: Pathfinder.

Castro, R. 1983. "Principles of People's Power." August 22, 1974. In *Fidel Castro's Speeches, Vol. II: Our Power Is That of the Working People,* ed. M. Taber. New York: Pathfinder.

Chao, Z. 1984. "Chinese Health Care." In *Modern Chinese Medicine: A Comprehensive Review of Medicine in the People's Republic of China*, vol. 3, ed. W. He-guang and L. De-cheng. Boston: MIP Press.

Chilcote, R.A. 1991. "Alternative Approaches to Comparative Politics." In *New Directions in Comparative Politics*, rev., ed. H.J. Wiarda. Boulder, Colo.: Westview.

Chin, R., and A.S. Chin. 1969. *Psychological Research in Communist China, 1949–1966.* Cambridge, Mass.: MIT Press.

Clark, R. 1973. *The Book of Health: A Medical Encyclopedia for Everyone*, 3rd ed. New York: Van Nostrand Reinhold.

Codina Jiménez, A. 1987. "Worker Incentives in Cuba." *World Development* 15(1):127–38.

Connolly, W.E. 1987. *Politics and Ambiguity*. Madison: University of Wisconsin Press.

Connor, W. 1971. *Deviance in Soviet Society: Crime, Delinquency and Alcoholism.* New York: Columbia University Press.

Cravens, H. 1985. "Child Saving in the Age of Professionalism, 1915–1930." In *American Childhood: A Research Guide*, ed. J. Hawes and R. Hiner. Westport, Conn.: Greenwood.

Cros-Sandoval, M. 1986. *Mariel and Cuban National Identity*. Miami: Editorial SIBI.

Cuba Update. 1992. "The Fourth Party Congress." *Cuba Update* (April):13–23.

Cuban American National Foundation. 1988. *A Public Survey on the Quality of Health Care in the Province of Holguín, Cuba: A Confidential Report by the Cuban Communist Party.* Havana: Secretariat of the PCC.

Cura Morales, R. 1981. Algunas Consideraciones Acerca de la Típico-Social y lo Individual en la Personalidad en Situaciones de Indisciplina Escolar." *Boletín de Psicología* 4(2):59–78.

———. 1983. "Estudio Preliminar del Nivel de Discriminación y Confiabilidad de la Variante Indirecto del Método de Investigación de Actitudes (MIA) para Estudiantes de Nivel Medio y Pre-Universitario." *Boletín de Psicología* 6(1):37–53.

Danielson, R. 1979. *Cuban Medicine*. New Brunswick, N.J.: Transaction.

De la Caridad Martín Martín, M., J. Torres, L. Asén, and S. Ramos. 1986. "Aspectos Psicosociales Relacionados con la Interrupción del Embarazo." *Boletín de Psicología* 9(3):58–76.

De Montagu, G. 1949. "Judicial Organization in Cuba." *Judicature* 32:166–70.

Debray, R. 1967. *Revolution in the Revolution?* New York: Monthly Review.

Decreto-Ley Numero 32 Sobre la Disciplina Laboral. 1980. *Trabajadores* (February 21):3.

Decreto-Ley Numero 36 Sobre la Disciplina de Directores y Administradores. 1982. *Trabajadores* (March 11):3.

Decreto-Ley Numero 113 Sobre la Disciplina de los Centros Asistenciales del Sistema Nacional de Salud. 1989. *Gaceta Oficial de la República de Cuba* (March 6):51–55.

Del Pino, R. 1987. *General del Pino Speaks: An Insight into Elite Corruption and Military Dissension in Castro's Cuba.* Washington, D.C.: Cuban American National Foundation.

Desnoes, E. 1967. *Inconsolable Memories of Underdevelopment*. Cambridge, Mass.: MIT Press.

D'Estéfano Pisani, M. 1991. "International Law and U.S.-Cuban Relations." In *U.S.-Cuban Relations in the 1990s*, ed. J. Domínguez and R. Hernández. Boulder, Colo.: Westview.

Díaz Briquets, S. 1983. *The Health Revolution in Cuba*. Austin: University of Texas Press.

Díaz Briquets, S. and J. Pérez-López. 1989. "Internationalist Civilian Assistance: The Cuban Presence in Sub-Saharan Africa." In *Cuban Internationalism in Sub-Saharan Africa*, ed. S. Díaz Briquets. Pittsburgh: Duquesne University Press.

Domínguez, J.I. 1978. *Cuba: Order and Revolution*. Cambridge, Mass.: Belknap.

———. 1979. "A Reply to Azicri." *Cuban Studies* 9(2):78–81.

———. 1988. "Blaming Itself, Not Himself: Cuba's Political Regime After the Third Party Congress." In *Socialist Cuba: Past Interpretations, Future Challenges*, ed. S. Roca. Boulder, Colo.: Westview.

———. 1989a. "The Cuban Armed Forces, the Party and Society in Wartime and During Rectification (1986–1988)." *Journal of Communist Studies* 5(4):45–62.

———. 1989b. *To Make a World Safe for Revolution: Cuba's Foreign Policy*. Cambridge, Mass.: Harvard University Press.

Domínguez Acosta, L. 1989. "El Colectivo Laboral y el Joven." *Revista Cubana de Psicología* 6(1):51.

Domínguez García, L. 1989. "Estudio de Algunos Componentes del la Esfera Motivacional en Estudiantes Universitarios." *Revista Cubana de Psicología* 6(3):181–87.

Donahue, J.W. 1963. *Jesuit Education: An Essay on the Foundations of Its Ideas*. New York: Fordham University Press.

Donnelly, J. 1989. "Repression and Development: The Political Contingency of Human Rights Trade-offs." In *Human Rights and Development*, ed. D.P. Forsythe. New York: St. Martin's.

Ebon, M. 1967. *Che: The Making of a Legend*. New York: Universe.

Eckstein, S. 1982. "Structural and Ideological Bases of Cuba's Overseas Policy." *Politics and Society* 1:95–121.

———. 1988. "Why Cuban Internationalism?" In *Cuban Political Economy*, ed. A. Zimbalist. Boulder, Colo.: Westview.

———. 1990. "The Rectification of Errors or the Errors of the Rectification Process in Cuba?" *Cuban Studies* 20:67–85.

Elkonin, D.B. 1971. "Development of Speech." In *The Psychology of Preschool Children*, ed. A.V. Zaporozhets and D.B. Elkonin. Cambridge, Mass.: MIT Press.

Elkonin, D.B., A.V. Zaporozhets, and V.P. Zinchenko. 1971. "Development of Thinking." In *The Psychology of PreSchool Children*, ed. A.V. Zaporozhets and D.B. Elkonin. Cambridge, Mass.: MIT Press.

Elster, J. 1991. "Local Justice and Interpersonal Comparisons." In *Interpersonal Comparisons of Well-Being*, ed. J. Elster and J. Roemer. New York: Cambridge University Press.

Elster, J., and J. Roemer, eds. 1991. *Interpersonal Comparisons of Well-Being*. New York: Cambridge University Press.

Erisman, M.H. 1985. *Cuba's International Relations: The Anatomy of a Nationalistic Foreign Policy*. Boulder, Colo.: Westview.

Espín, V. 1991. *Cuban Women Confront the Future*, ed. D. Shnookal. Melbourne: Ocean.

Eveleth, P. 1986. "Population Differences in Growth: Environmental and Genetic Factors." In *Human Growth, Vol. 3: Methodology*, ed. F. Falkner and J.M. Tanner. New York: Plenum.

Evenson, D. 1986a. "Economic Regulation in Cuba: The State Arbitration System." *Loyola of Los Angeles International and Comparative Law Journal* 8(3):371–98.

———. 1986b. "Women's Equality in Cuba: What Difference Does a Revolution Make?" *Law and Inequality* 4(2):295–326.

———. 1990. "The Changing Role of Law in Revolutionary Cuba." In *Transformation and Struggle: Cuba Faces the 1990s*, ed. S. Halebsky and J.M. Kirk. New York: Praeger.

Fagen, R. 1965. "Charismatic Authority and the Leadership of Fidel Castro." *Western Political Quarterly* 18:275–84.

———. 1969. *The Transformation of Political Culture in Cuba*. Palo Alto, Calif.: Stanford University Press.

Family Code of the Republic of Cuba of 1975. 1980. *Review of Socialist Law* 6(2):217–45.

Federal Broadcast Information Service (FBIS). 1986. "Castro's Speech at Genetic Engineering Center," FBIS VI (July 7):2–12.

———.1990a. "Human Rights Association Members Interviewed," FBIS-LAT-90-140 (July 20):10–11.

———. 1990b. "Highlights of Castro's Address to the ANPP," FBIS-LAT-90-144 (July 26):7–15.

———. 1990c. "Labor Councils Replaced by 'New Experience,'" FBIS-LAT-90-155 (August 10):2–3.

———. 1990d. "ANPP President Discusses People's Government," FBIS-LAT-90-170 (August 31):5–15.

———. 1990e. "Castro Marks Blas Roca Contingent Anniversary," FBIS-LAT-90-193 (October 4):1–6.

———. 1990f. "Party Makes Leadership, Organizational Changes," FBIS-LAT-90-195 (October 9):3–4.

———. 1990g. "Castro, People's Council Leaders Discuss Tasks," FBIS-LAT-90-198 (October 12):2–3.

———. 1991a. "Castro Addresses Close of Health Conference," FBIS-LAT-91-056 (March 22):2–14.

———. 1991b. "CDR Secretariat Announces Restructuring Process," FBIS-LAT-91-057 (March 25):6–7.

———. 1991c. "Sociologist Reports on 'Underground Capitalism,'" FBIS-LAT-91-059 (March 27):7–8.

———. 1991d. "Practice of Bribery, Sanctions Discussed," FBIS-LAT-91-100 (May 23):3–4.

———. 1991e. "Citizens Urged to Report Illicit Activities," FBIS-LAT-91-104 (May 30):2–4.

————. 1991f. "New Labor Regulations Further Explained," FBIS-LAT-91-105 (May 31):6–7.

————. 1991g. "Physicians Found Guilty of Anti-Castro Plot," FBIS-LAT-91-124 (June 27):2–3.

————. 1991h. "Health Organization Inaugurates New Offices," FBIS-LAT-91-216 (November 7):12–13.

————. 1991i. "Scientific Communities Under Construction," FBIS-LAT-91-219 (November 13):4.

Feinsilver, J. 1989a. "Cuba as a 'World Medical Power': The Politics of Symbolism." *Latin American Research Review* 24(2):1–35.

————. 1989b. "Symbolic Politics and Health Policy: Cuba as a 'World Medical Power.'" Ph.D. diss., Yale University.

Fernández González, A.M. 1987. "Las Relaciones Interpersonales en Grupos de Estudiantes." *Boletín de Psicología* 10(2):42–55.

Field, M. 1991a. "Soviet Health Problems and the Convergence Hypothesis." In *Soviet Social Problems*, ed. A. Jones, W.D. Connor, and D.E. Powell. Boulder, Colo.: Westview Press.

————. 1991b. "The Hybrid Profession: Soviet Medicine." In *Professions and the State: Expertise and Autonomy in the Soviet State*, ed. A. Jones. Philadelphia: Temple University Press.

Finlay, O. 1981. "The Rights of Children in Cuba." *Columbia Human Rights Review* 12:221–62.

Fishbein, M., ed. 1967. *Readings in Attitude Theory and Measurement.* New York: Wiley.

Fitzgerald, F.T. 1989. "The Reform of the Cuban Economy, 1976–1986: Organization, Incentives, and Patterns of Behavior." *Journal of Latin American Studies* 21:283–310.

————. 1990a. "Cuba's New Professionals." In *Transformation and Struggle: Cuba Faces the 1990s*, ed. S. Halebsky and J.M. Kirk. New York: Praeger.

————. 1990b. *Managing Socialism: From Old Cadres to New Professionals in Revolutionary Cuba.* Westport, Conn.: Greenwood.

Foucault, M. 1973. *The Birth of the Clinic: An Archaeology of Medical Perception.* New York: Vintage.

————. 1978. *The History of Sexuality, Volume I: An Introduction.* New York: Vintage.

————. 1979. *Discipline and Punish.* New York: Vintage.

————. 1980. "Two Lectures." In *Power and Knowledge*, ed. C. Gordon. New York: Pantheon.

————. 1982. "The Subject and Power." In *Michel Foucault: Beyond Structuralism and Hermeneutics*, ed. H. Dreyfus and P. Rabinow. Chicago: University of Chicago Press.

Freidson, E. 1986. *Professional Powers: The Study of the Institutionalization and Formalization of Knowledge.* Chicago: University of Chicago Press.

Fuentes Avila, M. 1982. "Nivel de Desarrollo del Grupo, Cohesión Grupal y la Actitud Hacia la Actividad Conjunta, Su Influencia en el Rendimiento Grupal." *Revista del Hospital Psiquiátrico de la Habana* 23:121–25.

Fuller, L. 1985. "The Politics of Worker's Control in Cuba, 1959–1983: The Work Center and the National Arena." Ph.D. diss., University of California, Berkeley.

———. 1988. "Fieldwork in Forbidden Terrain: The U.S. State and the Case of Cuba." *American Sociologist* 19(2):99–120.

———. 1992. *Work and Democracy in Socialist Cuba.* Philadelphia: Temple University Press.

Galanter, M. 1966. "The Modernization of Law." In *Modernization and the Dynamics of Growth,* ed. N. Weiner. New York: Basic.

García-Averasturi, L. 1980. "Psychology and Health Care in Cuba." *American Psychologist* 35(12):1090–95.

———. 1985. "Community Health Psychology in Cuba." *Journal of Community Psychology* 13(2):111–23.

———. 1988. "Psychological Factors and Health: The Cuban Model." In *Health and Cross-Cultural Psychology,* ed. P.R. Deser and J.W. Berry. Beverly Hills, Calif.: Sage.

García-Crews, A. 1988. "Human Rights in Cuba: Report of a Delegation of the Association of the Bar of the City of New York." *University of Miami Inter-American Law Review* 20:207–48.

García Márquez, G. 1990. "Fidel's Tale." *Spin* 6(6):46–51.

Gevins, A.S., and A. Rémond, eds. 1987. *Handbook of Electroencephalography and Clinical Neurophysiology, Vol. I: Methods of Analysis of Brain Electrical and Magnetic Signals.* Amsterdam: Elsevier.

Giffard, A.C. 1989. *UNESCO and the Media.* New York: Longman.

Gillette, H. 1973. "Military Occupation of Cuba, 1899–1902: Workshop for American Progressivism." *American Quarterly* 25(4):410–25.

Gilpin, M. 1978. "Focus on Mental Health Care." *Cuba Review* 8:31–32.

Gilpin, M., and H. Rodríguez-Trias. 1978. "Looking at Health in a Healthy Way." *Cuba Review* 8:3–15.

Goldstein, H. 1986. "Sampling for Growth Studies." In *Human Growth, Vol. III: Methodology,* ed. F. Falkner and J.M. Tanner. New York: Plenum.

Gómez, U.R., F.U. Ramos, and J.R. Lauzurique. 1989. "Sistema Psicomet para la Automatización del Diagnóstico Psycológico." *Revista Cubana de Psicología* 6(1):5–9.

González, E. 1976. "Political Succession in Cuba." *Studies in Comparative Communism* 9:80–107.

———. 1979. "Institutionalization, Political Elites and Foreign Policy." In *Cuba in the World,* ed. C. Blasier and C. Mesa-Lago. Pittsburgh: University of Pittsburgh Press.

González Delgado, J.B. 1983. "Biorritmo y Mortalidad Fetal." *Boletín de Psicología* 6(2):35–43.

González Menéndez, R. et al. 1984. "Criterios Sobre la Educación Formal y Su Significación Profesional: Resultados de una Encuesta a Estudiantes de Medicina." *Boletín de Psicología* 7(3):122.

González Pacheco, O. 1982. "La Autorregulación Moral del Comportamiento." *Revista del Hospital Psiquiátrico de la Habana* 23:87–139.

González Rey, F.L. 1986. "Las Operaciones Cognitivas de la Personalidad." *Revista Cubana de Psicología* 3(3):81.

———. 1987. "La Categoría Actitud en la Psicología." *Revista Cubana de Psicología* 4(1):47–59.

———. 1988. "La Psicología: Reflexiones Sobre Su Lugar in el Campo de la Salud" *Revista Cubana de Psicología* 5(3):55–60.

González Serra, D.J., and A. Alonso Alvárez. 1983. "Motivational Study of Mental Illness." *Revista del Hospital Psiquiátrico de la Habana* 23:141–55.

Goodsell, J.N. 1967. "Castro Support Seems Rooted Among Youth." *Christian Science Monitor* (August 22):20.

Goodsell, J.N., and O. Gutiérrez López. 1986. "Imagen Ideal del Médico en Estudiantes de Medicina de Primero y Segundo Años." *Boletín de Psicología* 9(1):80–93.

Gozá León, J. 1982. "Relación Médico-Paciente en la Clínica de Algunas Enfermedades Psicosomáticas (Asma Bronquial y Úcera Gastroduodenal)." *Boletín de Psicología* 5(2):114–32.

———. 1983. "Vigencia y Permanencia de la Relación Médico-Paciente." *Boletín de Psicología* 6(1):61–85.

Gozá León, J., and O. Gutiérrez López. 1986. "Imagen Ideal del Médico en Estudiante de Medicina del Primero y Segundo Años: Estudio Exploratorio." *Boletín de Psicología* 9(1):80–93.

Granma Weekly Review. 1970. "Without Socialism There Cannot Be Any Development in an Underdeveloped Country." *Granma Weekly Review* (December 28):6–10.

———. 1982. "Fidel Meets with the First Contingent of the Carlos J. Finlay Medical Sciences Detachment." *Granma Weekly Review* (January 17):1–5.

———. 1985. "Speech by Fidel Castro Given to the Fourth Congress of the Federation of Cuban Women." *Granma Weekly Review* (March 8):2–10.

———. 1986a. "Excerpts from Castro's Remarks to National Assembly." *Granma Weekly Review* (January 12):4.

———. 1986b. "Fidel Speaks on the Family Doctor Program." *Granma Weekly Review* (June 8):4.

———. 1986c. "Fidel's Remarks During National Assembly Meeting: Labor, Discipline and Legislation." *Granma Weekly Review* (January 12):6.

———. 1986d. "Closing Remarks by Fidel Castro to the International Seminar on Primary Health Care, Havana." *Granma Weekly Review* (June 22):1.

———. 1987. "Speech on the Ceremony on the Twentieth Anniversary of the Death of Guevara." *Granma Weekly Review* (October 18):4–5.

———. 1989. "Havana Focal Point for Psychologists Next Year." *Granma Weekly Review* (May 28):4.

———. 1990a. "Fidel at Closing of the Sixteenth Congress of the Central Organization of Cuban Trade Unions." *Granma Weekly Review* (February 11):1–4.

———. 1990b. "Fidel Addresses Thirtieth Anniversary of CDRs." *Granma Weekly Review* (October 14):4–9.

———. 1990c. "Group of Measures Concerning Party Structure and Functioning Approved." *Granma Weekly Review* (October 14):9.

———. 1991. "Fidel's Closing Speech at the Eighth Regular Session of the National Assembly of People's Power." *Granma Weekly Review* (January 13): 2.

Grant, G. 1989. "The Family and Social Control: Traditional and Modern." In *Social Control in the People's Republic of China*, ed. R. Troyer, J. Clark, and D. Rojek. New York: Praeger.

Gray, J. 1991. "Post-Totalitarianism, Civil Society, and the Limits of the Western Model." In *The Reemergence of Civil Society in Eastern Europe and the Soviet Union*, ed. Z. Rau. Boulder, Colo.: Westview.

Grogg, P. 1991. "Crime and Counterrevolution." *Cuba Update* (November):30–32.

Guevara, C. 1968a. "On Revolutionary Medicine." Speech, August 19, 1960. In *Venceremos: The Speeches and Writings of Ernesto Che Guevara*, ed. J. Gerassi. New York: Macmillan.

———. 1968b. "Cuba—Exception or Vanguard?" Speech, April 9, 1961. In *Venceremos: The Speeches and Writings of Ernesto Che Guevara*, ed. J. Gerassi. New York: Macmillan.

———. 1968c. "On Being a Communist Youth." Speech, October 20, 1962. In *Venceremos: The Speeches and Writings of Ernesto Che Guevara*, ed. J. Gerassi. New York: Macmillan.

———. 1968d. "On Creating a New Attitude." Speech, August 15, 1964. In *Venceremos: The Speeches and Writings of Ernesto Che Guevara*, ed. J. Gerassi. New York: Macmillan.

———. 1968e. "Notes on Man in Socialism." Letter, 1965. In *Venceremos: The Speeches and Writings of Ernesto Che Guevara*, ed. J. Gerassi. New York: Macmillan.

———. 1985. *Guerrilla Warfare*. New York: Monthly Review.

Gusfield, J.R. 1967. "Tradition and Modernity: Misplaced Polarities in the Study of Change." *American Journal of Sociology* 72:351–62.

Habel, J. 1991. *Cuba: The Revolution in Peril*, trans. J. Barnes. New York: Verso.

Halebsky, S., and J.M. Kirk, eds. 1985. *Cuba: Twenty-Five Years of Revolution, 1959–1984*. New York: Praeger.

———. 1990. *Transformation and Struggle: Cuba Faces the 1990s*. New York: Praeger.

Hamberg, J. 1986. "The Dynamics of Cuban Housing Policy." In *Critical Perspectives on Housing*, ed. R. Bratt et al. Philadelphia: Temple University Press.

———. 1990. "Cuban Housing Policy." In *Transformation and Struggle: Cuba Faces the 1990s*, ed. S. Halebsky and J.M. Kirk. New York: Praeger.

Harmony, T. et al. 1973. "Symmetry of the Visual Evoked Potential in Normal Subjects." *Electoencephalography and Clinical Neurophysiology* 35:237–40.

Harmony, T., G. Otero, J. Ricardo, and G. Fernández. 1973. "Polarity Coincidence Correlation Coefficient and Signal Energy Ratio of the Ongoing EEG Activity." *Brain Research* 61:133–40.

Hayden, R.M. 1985. "Who Wants Informal Courts? Paradoxical Evidence from a Yugoslav Attempt to Create Workers' Courts for Labor Cases." *American Bar Foundation Research Journal* 23(2):293–326.

Hazard, J.H. 1969. *Communists and Their Law*. Chicago: University of Chicago Press.

Heitlinger, A. 1991. "Hierarchy of Status and Prestige Within the Medical Profession in Czechoslovakia." In *Professions and the State: Expertise and Autonomy in the Soviet Union and Eastern Europe*, ed. A. Jones. Philadelphia: Temple University Press.

Henkin, A. et al. 1988. "Human Rights in Cuba: Report of a Delegation of the Association of the Bar of the City of New York." *University of Miami Inter-American Law Review* 20:207–48.

Hernández de Aramas, N. 1977. "Las Causas del Delito." *Revista del Hospital Psiquiátrico de la Habana* 18:301–22.

Hernández Meléndez, D.E. 1984. "Creación y Validación de un Instrumento para la Evaluación de la Sugestionabilidad." *Boletín de Psicología* (Special edition):30–40.

Herrera Jiménez, L.F. 1988. "Estudio Comparativo del Desarrollo de los Procesos Cognoscitivos en Niños con Retardo en el Desarrollo Psíquico y Retraso Mental Ligero." *Boletín de Psicología* 11(1):121–37.

Herrera Jiménez, L.F., Y. Díaz Castillo et al. 1987. "Algunas Consideraciones Sobre Las Situaciones Que Comúnmente Generan Ansiedad Patológica y Su Relación con la Ansiedad Personal." *Boletín de Psicología* 10(3):3–76.

Herrera Jiménez, L.F. et al. 1987. "Estudio del Componente Operacional del Pensamiento en Pacientes con Síntomas Neuróticos." *Boletín de Psicología* 10(2):30–41.

Herrera Jiménez, L.F., E. Serret Mesa, and L. Morenza Paudilla. 1987. "Estudio de la Atención Voluntaria en Niños de Siete a Nueve Años de Edad con Retardo en el Desarrollo Psíquico." *Boletín de Psicología* 10(3):17–31.

Hjern, B., and C. Hull. 1982. "Implementation Research as Empirical Constitutionalism." *European Journal of Political Research* 10:105–15.

Horowitz, D. 1977. *The Courts and Social Policy*. Washington, D.C.: Brookings Institution.

Horowitz, I.L. 1979. "A Reply to Azicri." *Cuban Studies* 9(2):84–89.

Huntington, S.P. 1981. *American Politics: The Promise of Disharmony*. Cambridge, Mass.: Belknap.

Ilizástigui Pérez, I., and R.I. Ageenko. 1986. "Los Sistemas Expertos de Inteligencia Artifical y Sus Aplicaciones en la Medicina y la Psicología." *Boletín de Psicología* 9(3):30–36.

Irons, J. 1981. "The Relegalization of Cuba." *American Legal Studies Association* 5:520–36.

Isaiev, D.N. 1967. "Las Neurosis y Psicosis Psicogenícas y Su Análisis Fisiopatológico." *Revista del Hospital Psiquiátrico de la Habana* 8:489–510.

ISCM-H, Colectivo de Alumnos de Tercer Año de la Facultad de Medicina No. 1. 1981. "Cambios de Vida y Comienzo de Enfermedad." *Boletín de Psicología* 4(1):60–75.

John, E.R. 1977. *Neurometrics: Clinical Applications of Quantitative Electrophysiology*. New York: Wiley.

John, E.R., L.S. Prichep, J.S. Fridman, and P. Easton. 1988. "Neurometrics: Computer-Assisted Differential Diagnosis of Brain Dysfunctions." *Science* 239 (January 8):162–69.

Johnson, C., and B. Canon. 1984. *Judicial Policy: Implementation and Impact*. Washington, D.C.: Congressional Quarterly.

Jones, A., and E.A. Krause. 1991. "Professions, the State and the Reconstruction of Socialist Societies." In *Professions and the State: Expertise and Autonomy in the Soviet Union and Eastern Europe,* ed. A. Jones. Philadelphia: Temple University Press.

Jordan, J.R. 1979. *Desarrollo Humano en Cuba.* Havana: Instituto de la Infancia, Ministerio de Cultura, Editorial Cientifico-Technica.

Jordan, J.R. et al. 1975. "The 1972 Cuban National Child Growth Study as an Example of Population Health Monitoring: Design and Methods." *Journal of Human Biology* 2(2):153–71.

Kabrin, V., and A. Pérez Yera. 1984. "La Función de la Autovaloración en al Mecanismo Sociopsicológico de la Autorrealización de la Personalidad." *Boletín de Psicología* (Special edition):5–16.

Kahneman, D., and C. Varey. 1991. "Notes on the Psychology of Utility." In *Interpersonal Comparisons of Well-Being,* ed. J. Elster and J. Roemer. New York: Cambridge University Press.

Kaidanovskaia, A.I. 1982. "La Concientización de las Acciones como Problema de la Psicología del Pensamiento." *Revista del Hospital Psiquiátrico de la Habana* 23:597–606.

Kates, N. 1987. "Mental Health Services in Cuba." *Hospital and Community Psychiatry* 38(7):755–58.

Kennedy, I.M. 1973. "Cuba's Ley Contra la Vagrancia—The Law on Loafing." *UCLA Law Review* 20:1147–1256.

Kennedy, M.D., and K. Sadkowski. 1991. "Constraints on Professional Power in Soviet-Type Society: Insights from the 1980–1981 Solidarity Period in Poland." In *Professions and the State: Expertise and Autonomy in the Soviet Union and Eastern Europe,* ed. A. Jones. Philadelphia: Temple University Press.

Kenworthy, E. 1985. "Cuba's Experiment in Local Democracy." *Journal of Community Psychology* 13(2):194–203.

Kirk, J.T. 1983. *José Martí: Mentor of the Cuban Nation.* Tampa Bay: University Presses of Florida.

Kleinig, J. 1983. *Paternalism.* Totowa, N.J.: Rowman and Allanheld.

Knoke, D. 1990. *Political Networks: The Structural Perspective.* New York: Cambridge University Press.

Koningsberger, H. 1971. *The Future of Che Guevara.* Garden City, N.Y.: Doubleday.

Kouri, G.P., M.G. Guzman, J.R. Bravo, and C. Triana. 1989. "Dengue Haemorrhagic Fever/Dengue Shock Syndrome: Lessons from the Cuban Epidemic, 1981." *Bulletin of the World Health Organization* 67(4):375–80.

Kozol, J. 1980. "Literacy and the Underdeveloped Nations." *Journal of Education* 162(3):27–39.

Kozulin, A. 1984. *Psychology in Utopia: Towards a Social History of Soviet Psychology.* Cambridge, Mass.: MIT Press.

———. 1986. "The Concept of Activity in Soviet Psychology: Vygotsky, His Disciples and Critics." *American Psychologist* 41(3):264–74.

Krause, E.A. 1991. "Professions and the State in the Soviet Union and Eastern Europe: Theoretical Issues." In *Professions and the State: Expertise and Autonomy in the Soviet Union and Eastern Europe,* ed. A. Jones. Philadelphia: Temple University Press.

Krich, J. 1981. *A Totally Free Man: An Unauthorized Autobiography of Fidel Castro.* Berkeley, Calif.: Creative Arts.

Lambo, T.A. 1985. "Political, Cultural, Psychological and Economic Constraints on World Medical Progress." In *Medical Science and the Advancement of World Health*, ed. R. Lanza. New York: Praeger.

Lampton, D. 1987. "The Implementation Problem in Post-Mao China." In *Policy Implementation in Post-Mao China*, ed. D. Lampton. Berkeley and Los Angeles: University of California Press.

Lauzurique Hubbard, J.R. et al. 1983. "Determinación de las Varables Psicológicas Más Significativas en Pacientes Coronarios bajo Tensión Emocional que Van a Ser Sometidos a Monitereo Electrocardiográfico Ambulatorio." *Boletín de Psicología* 6(3):87–104.

Lee, H.Y. 1991. *From Revolutionary Cadres to Party Technocrats in Socialist China.* Berkeley and Los Angeles: University of California Press.

Leiner, M. 1987. "The 1961 National Cuban Literacy Campaign." In *National Literacy Campaigns: Historical and Comparative Perspectives*, ed. R. Arnove and H. Graff. New York: Plenum.

LeoGrande, W. 1978. "Continuity and Change in the Cuban Political Elite." *Cuban Studies* 8:1–31.

———. 1979. "The Theory and Practice of Socialist Democracy in Cuba: Mechanism of Elite Accountability." *Studies of Comparative Communism* 12(1):39–62.

Lerman, P. 1982. *Deinstitutionalization and the Welfare State.* New Brunswick, N.J.: Rutgers University Press.

Lewis, J.W. 1986. *Political Networks and the Chinese Policy Process.* Occasional Paper of the Northeast Asia–United States Forum on International Policy. Palo Alto, Calif.: Stanford University.

Lewis, O. 1977a. *Living the Revolution: Four Men.* Urbana: University of Illinois Press.

———. 1977b. *Living the Revolution: Four Women.* Urbana: University of Illinois Press.

Limonta Vidal, M., and G. Padrón. 1991. "The Development of High Technology and Its Medical Applications in Cuba." *Latin American Perspectives* 18(2): 101–13.

Livingston, M., and P. Lowinger. 1983. *The Minds of the Chinese People: Mental Health in the New China.* Englewood Cliffs, N.J.: Prentice-Hall.

Llano, B. 1977. "Psiquiatría en la Comunidad." *Revista del Hospital Psiquiátrico de la Habana* 18:27–38.

Lockmiller, D. 1937. "The Advisory Law Commission of Cuba." *Hispanic American Historical Review* 19:2–29.

Lowenthal, A.S., B.B. Lowenthal, and C. Danson. 1985. "Psychology and Human Services in Cuba: Personal Perspectives." *Journal of Community Psychology* 13(2):105–16.

MacIntyre, A. 1988. *Whose Justice, Which Rationality?* South Bend, Ind.: University of Notre Dame Press.

Marin, B. 1985. "Community Psychology in Cuba: A Literature Review." *Journal of Community Psychology* 13(2):138–54.

Marin, G. 1988. "Cuba." In *International Handbook of Psychology.* Westport, Conn.: Greenwood.

Marsden, P., and N. Lin, eds. 1982. *Social Structure and Network Analysis*. Beverly Hills, Calif.: Sage.

Martz, J.D. 1991. "Bureaucratic-Authoritarianism, Transitions to Democracy, and the Political-Culture Dimension," In *New Directions in Comparative Politics*, rev., ed. H.J. Wiarda. Boulder, Colo.: Westview.

Mathéy, K. 1989. "Recent Trends in Housing Policies in Cuba and the Revival of the Microbrigade Movement." *Bulletin of Latin American Research* 8:67–81.

McCormick, B.L. 1987. "Leninist Implementation: The Election Campaign." In *Policy Implementation in Post-Mao China*, ed. D. Lampton. Berkeley and Los Angeles: University of California Press.

McGraw, M.B. 1943. *The Neuromuscular Maturation of the Human Infant*. New York: Columbia University Press.

Medin, T. 1990. *Cuba: The Shaping of Revolutionary Consciousness*. Boulder, Colo.: Lynne Rienner.

Méndez Martínez, R., L. Pérez Rodríguez, and D.A. Martínez Brunet. 1986. "El Médico de la Familia y el Componente Sociopsicológico de la Antención Integral." *Boletín de Psicología* 9(2):17–48.

Mesa-Lago, C. 1968. *The Labor Sector and Social Distribution in Cuba*. New York: Hoover Institution.

———. 1978. *Cuba in the 1970s: Pragmatism and Institutionalization*, rev. Albuquerque: University of New Mexico Press.

———. 1981. *The Economy of Socialist Cuba: A Two Decade Appraisal*. Albuquerque: University of New Mexico Press.

———. 1989. "Cuba's Economic Counter-Reform (*Rectificación*): Causes, Policies and Effects." *Journal of Communist Studies* 5(4):98–139.

Millar, J. 1988. "The Little Deal: Brezhnev's Contribution to Acquisitive Socialism." In *Soviet Society and Culture*, ed. T. Thompson and R. Sheldon. Boulder, Colo.: Westview.

Miller, J.A. 1986. "Cuba's Commitment to Genetic Engineering Grows in Size and Scope." *Genetic Engineering News* (May):22–23.

Mina, G. 1991. *An Encounter with Fidel*, trans. M. Todd. Melbourne: Ocean.

Mitjans Martínez, A., and M. Febles Elejaldes. 1983. "Social Function of the Psychologist in Cuba." *Revista del Hospital Psiquiátrico de la Habana* 23:5–20.

Molina Avilés, J. 1986. "Crónica del XX Congreso Interamericano de Psicología." *Revista Cubana de Psicología* 3(2):3–6.

Nelson, H. 1991. "Overmedicated? An Excess of Success May Ail Cuba's Top-Flight Health Care System." *Cuba Update* (November):33–34.

Nikelly, A.C. 1987. "Prevention in Sweden and Cuba: Implications for Policy Research." *Journal of Primary Prevention* 7(3):117–31.

Nydia Ramos, A., and González-Rey, F. 1986. "Hacia una Nueva Comprensión de la Personalidad Humana: Implicaciones y Pespectivas para la Psicología Latinoamericana." *Revista Cubana de Psicología* 3(2):7–14.

O'Brien, K. 1990. *Reform Without Liberalization: China's National People's Congress and the Politics of Institutional Change*. New York: Cambridge University Press.

Oleszczuk, T.A. 1988. *Political Justice in the USSR: Dissent and Repression in Lithuania, 1969–1987*. New York: Columbia University Press.

Ojalvo Mitrani, V., and G. Mijailovna Andreieva. 1981. "Influencia de los Valores de los Adultos y los Contemporñeos en el Respeto a las Normas Sociales en la Conducta 'Verbal' y 'Real' del Adolescente." *Boletín de Psicología* 4(2):79–100.

Ordaz Ducungé, E. 1983. "Palabras del Director." *Revista del Hospital Psiquiátrico de la Habana* 24:1–72.

Ortíz Torres, E., T. Díaz Fernández, and A. Grimal Zayas. 1987. "La Crítica por Niveles a la Psicología Burguesa Contemporánea en Algunos Contenidos de Psicología General." *Revista Cubana de Psicología* 4(1):85–100.

Peña Betancurt, M. et. al. 1987. "Miocariopatia Familiar. Estudio Psicológico." *Boletín de Psicología* 10(1):23–37.

Pérez Lovelle, R. 1985. "La Personalidad y las Características Generales de Su Actividad." *Boletín de Psicología* 8(2):87–113.

Pérez Rodríguez, G.L. 1982. "El Lenguaje y la Actividad Práctica en el Desarrollo del Pensamiento Calsificatorio del Niño." *Boletín de Psicología* 5(3):51–66.

Pérez Vera, A. 1984. "Confección de un Modelo para el Análisis del Nivel de Desarrollo de los Colectivos." *Boletín de Psicología* 7(4):61–70.

Pérez-López, J.F. 1987. *Measuring Cuban Economic Performance*. Austin: University of Texas Press.

Pérez-Stable, E.J. 1985. "Community Medicine in Cuba." *Journal of Community Psychology* 13(2):124–37.

Pérez-Stable, M. 1986. *Politics and Conscience in Twentieth Century Society: The Cuban Experience*. Old Westbury, N.Y.: State University of New York.

———. 1990. "In Pursuit of Cuba Libre." *North American Congress on Latin America: Report on the Americas* 24(2):23–31.

Platt, A. 1988. "Cuba and Human Rights." *Social Justice* 15(2):38–54.

Portero Cabrera, D.R. 1984. "Estudio Exploratorio de la Ansiedad Patológica en Adolescentes." *Boletín de Psicología* (Special edition):92–100.

Portes, A. 1973. "Modernity and Development: A Critique." *Studies in Comparative International Development* 8(3):247–78.

Preston, J. 1989. "Castro's Purge Trial." *New York Review of Books* 36(19):24–31.

Quintana Mendoza, J.D., C. González Rodríguez, J. Antonio Espinel, and N. Pérez Valdéz. 1984. "Personalidad Normal, Personalidad Inadecuada: Un Estudio Comparativo de Actitudes." *Boletín de Psicología* 7(1):89–94.

Rabkin, R. 1987. "Cuba." In *International Handbook of Human Rights*, ed. J. Donnelly and R. Howard. Westport, Conn.: Greenwood.

———. 1988. "Cuba: The Aging of the Revolution." In *Socialist Cuba: Past Interpretations and Future Challenges*, ed. S. Roca. Boulder, Colo.: Westview.

———. 1991. *Cuban Politics: The Revolutionary Experiment*. New York: Praeger.

Rau, Z. 1991. "Introduction." In *The Reemergence of Civil Society in Eastern Europe and the Soviet Union*, ed. Z. Rau. Boulder, Colo.: Westview.

Reed, G., ed. 1992. *Island in the Storm: The Cuban Communist Party's Fourth Congress*. Melbourne: Ocean.

Reyes Gutiérrez, B.R., and M. Simón Consuegra. 1987. "Influencia del Biorrithmo en las Psicosis Maniaco-Depresiva." *Boletín de Psicología* 10(3):49–63.

Riera Milián, M.A. 1987. "Análisis del Comportamiento Emocional bajo la Influencia de los Efectos de Frustración y Tensión Psíquica, Provocada Experimentalmente en Atletas de los Equipos de Softball Femenino y Masculino." *Boletín de Psicología* 10(2):111–22.

Ritter, A.R.M. 1988. "The Organs of People's Power and the Communist Party: The Nature of Cuban Democracy." In *Cuba: Twenty-Five Years of Revolution, 1959–1984,* ed. S. Halebsky and J.M. Kirk. New York: Praeger.

Riveron, R., H. Ferrer García, and F. Valdéz Lazo. 1976. "Advances in Pediatrics and Child Care in Cuba." *Pan American Health Organization Bulletin* 10(1): 9–24.

Roca Perara, M.A., G.M. Ángel Yero, P.E. Moras, and C. Sánchez. 1982. "Estudio de los Ideales Morales en Jovenes Transgresores." *Revista del Hospital Psiquiátrico de la Habana* 23:127–39.

Roett, R. 1984. *Brazil: Politics in a Patrimonial Society,* 3rd ed. New York: Praeger.

Rojek, D.G. 1989. "Confucianism, Maoism, and the Coming of Delinquency to China." In *Social Control in the People's Republic,* ed. R. Troyer, J.P. Clark, and D.G. Rojek. New York: Praeger.

Román Hernández, J., P. Almirall Hernández, J.P. González Castaño, and C. Comellas Fernández. 1985. "Variables Psicológicos Asociadas a la Exposición a Ruidos y Vibraciones." *Boletín de Psicología* 8(3):131.

Sabatier, P. 1986. "Top-Down and Bottom-Up Approaches to Implementation Research: A Critical Analysis and Suggested Synthesis." *Journal of Public Policy* 6(1):21–48.

Salas, L. 1979a. "Juvenile Delinquency in Post-Revolutionary Cuba." *Cuban Studies* 9(1):43–59.

———. 1979b. *Social Control and Deviance in Cuba.* New York: Praeger.

———. 1983. "The Emergence and Decline of the Cuban Popular Tribunals." *Law and Society Review* 17(4):586–612.

Sampson, S. 1985. "The Informal Sector in Eastern Europe." *Telos* 66:44–66.

Santana, S. 1987. "The Cuban Health Care System." *World Development* 15(1): 113–25.

———. 1990. "Whither Cuban Medicine? Challenges for the Next Generation." In *Transformation and Struggle: Cuba Faces the 1990s,* ed. S. Halebsky and J.M. Kirk. New York: Praeger.

Sasson, A. 1984. *Biotechnologies: Challenges and Promises.* New York: UNESCO.

———. 1988. *Biotechnologies and Development.* Paris: UNESCO.

Schanche, D.A. 1989. "Cuban Rights Crackdown, Psychiatric Abuses Told." *Los Angeles Times* (January 12):1, 13.

Scheingold, S. 1974. *The Politics of Rights: Lawyers, Public Policy and Political Change.* New Haven, Conn.: Yale University Press.

Schlesinger, Jr., A. 1992. "Four Days with Fidel: A Havana Diary." *New York Review of Books* 39(6):22–28.

Sección Estudiantil. 1982. "Relación Médico-Paciente: Su Utilización por Estudiantes de Medicina." *Boletín de Psicología* 5(1):95–103.

Sharlet, R. 1978. "Pashukanis and the Withering Away of Law in the USSR." In *The Cultural Revolution in Russia, 1928–1931,* ed. S. Fitzpatrick. Bloomington: Indiana University Press.

Shaw, K. 1982. "Youth in Trouble." *Cuba Times* (January-February):23–26.

Shelley, L.I. 1984. *Lawyers in Soviet Work Life.* New Brunswick, N.J.: Rutgers University Press.

Shlapentokh, V. 1989. *Public and Private Life of the Soviet People.* New York: Oxford University Press.

Solé Arrondo, M.E. 1987. "El Problema de la Determinación: Condiciones Internas y Esternas del Desarrollo de la Personalidad." *Boletín de Psicología* 10(2):7–16.

Solomon, P. 1978. *Soviet Criminologists and Criminal Policy: Specialists in Policy-making.* New York: Columbia University Press.

Sosa Cardentey, C., and B. Martínez Perigod. 1984. "Uso de los Métodos Directos e Indirectos en el Conocimiento de la Motivación de los Adolescentes con Conducta Social Desviada." *Boletín de Psicología* 7(1):22–37.

Stein, Z., and M. Susser. 1972. "The Cuban Health System." *International Journal of Health Services* 2(4):551–66.

Stromas, A. 1979. "Dissent and Policy Change in the Soviet Union." *Studies in Comparative Communism* 12(2):212–44.

Szelenyi, I. 1988. *Socialist Entrepreneurs: Embourgeoisement in Hungary.* Madison: University of Wisconsin Press.

Tanner, J.M. 1963. "The Regulation of Human Growth." *Child Development* 34:817–47.

———. 1986. "Growth as a Target-Seeking Function." In *Human Growth: A Comprehensive Treatise,* 2nd ed., ed. F. Falkner and J.M. Tanner. New York: Plenum.

Tesh, S. 1986. "Health Education in Cuba: A Reform." *International Journal of Health* 16(1):87–104.

———. 1988. *Hidden Arguments: Political Ideology and Disease Prevention.* New Brunswick, N.J.: Rutgers University Press.

Tesoro, S. 1990. "A Pecho Descubierto." *Bohemia* (June 20):50–55.

Thelen, E. 1990. "Dynamical Systems and the Generation of Individual Differences." In *Individual Differences in Infancy,* ed. J. Columbo and J. Fager. Hillsdale, N.J.: Erlbaum.

Thelen, E., and B.D. Ulrich. 1991. *Hidden Skills,* Monographs of the Society for Research in Child Development, Vol. 56, Serial 223, No. 1. Chicago: University of Chicago Press.

Theobald, R. 1990. *Corruption, Development and Underdevelopment.* Durham, N.C.: Duke University Press.

Torres Páez, T., and M. Alonso Cruz. 1989. "Algunas Consideraciones Sobre la Formación de Actitudes ante el Estudio y la Profesión en Jóvenes." *Revista Cubana de Psicología* 6(2):69–78.

Torroella, G. 1966. "Los Padres y la Orientación de los Hijos." *Bohemia* (January 14):16–20.

———. 1968. "El Problema de la Disciplina del Niño." *Bohemia* (August 9):14–21.

Troyer, R.J. 1989. "Chinese Social Organization." In *Social Control in the People's Republic of China,* ed. R.J. Troyer et. al. New York: Praeger.

Turk, A.T. 1989. "Political Deviance and Popular Justice in China: Lessons for the West." In *Social Control in the People's Republic of China.* New York: Praeger.

Ubell, R.N. 1983a. "Cuba's Great Leap: Cuba May Be Moving into the Big League of Scientific Nations at Just the Right Time." *Nature* 302 (April 28):745–48.

———. 1983b. "High Tech Medicine in the Caribbean." *New England Journal of Medicine* 30:923.

Unger, R. 1987. *False Necessity, Part I: Politics, a Work in Constructive Social Theory.* New York: Cambridge University Press.

Uria, M. et al. 1984. "Criterios para Abordar el Estudio de la Personalidad Desde el Punto de Vista Clínico." *Boletín de Psicología* (Special edition):101.

Valdéz, N.P. 1979. "A Reply to Azicri." *Cuban Studies* 9(2):81–84.

———. 1988. "Revolution and Paradigms: A Critical Assessment of Cuban Studies." In *Cuban Political Economy*, ed. A. Zimbalist. Boulder, Colo.: Westview.

Valdéz, N.P., and M.C. Montalvo. 1985. "Psychological Rehabilitation of the Chronic Mental Patient." *Journal of Community Psychology* 13(2):155–61.

Valdés Marín, R. 1980. "La Representación de los Animales en los Dibujos Infantiles." *Boletín de Psicología* 3(3–4):44–50.

———. 1983. "La Expressión Gráfica Infantil en Psicología Normal y Patológica." *Boletín de Psicología* 6(2):55–67.

Valsiner, J. 1988. *Developmental Psychology in the Soviet Union*. Bloomington: Indiana University Press.

Van der Plas, A. 1987. *Revolution and Criminal Justice: The Cuban Experiment, 1959–1983*. Amsterdam: CEDLA.

Vasallo Barrueta, N. 1986. "La Influencia del Micromedio Social en el Cumplimiento de las Medidas Criminológicas Individuales." *Revista Cubana de Psicología* 3(3):73–80.

Veitía Mora, S., E. Romero Monteagudo, and G. Lara Morel. 1984. "Vias para el Desarrollo de la Personalidad y Su Importancia Clínica y Educativa." *Boletín de Psicología* 7(3):85–94.

Vellinga, M.L. 1976. "The Military and the Dynamics of the Cuban Revolutionary Process." *Comparative Politics* 8(1):245–69.

Wald, K. 1978. *Children of Che*. Palo Alto, Calif.: Ramparts.

Walsh, M.W. 1992. "A Big Dose of Family Medicine." *Los Angeles Times* (July 16):1, 18–19.

Werner, D. 1980. *Health Care in Cuba Today: A Model Service or a Means of Social Control—or Both*. Palo Alto, Calif.: Hesperian Foundation.

White, T. 1987. "Implementing the 'One Child per Couple' Population Program in Rural China: National Goals and Local Politics." In *Policy Implementation in Post-Mao China*, ed. D. Lampton. Berkeley and Los Angeles: University of California Press.

Wiarda, H.J. 1971. "Law and Political Development in Latin America." *American Journal of Comparative Law* 19:434–63.

———. 1991. "Toward a Nonethnocentric Theory of Development: Alternative Conceptions from the Third World." In *New Directions in Comparative Politics*, rev., ed. H.J. Wiarda. Boulder, Colo.: Westview.

Wiatr, J. 1989. "The Civic Culture from a Marxist-Sociological Perspective." In *The Civil Culture Revisited*, ed. G. Almond and S. Verba. Newbury Park, Calif.: Sage.

Willerton, J.P. 1992. *Patronage and Politics in the USSR*. New York: Cambridge University Press.

Yang, M.M. 1989. "The Gift Economy and State Power in China." *Comparative Studies of Society and History* 31:25–54.

Zeigarnik, B.V., and V.V. Nicolaeva. 1981. "Lugar de la Psicología en la Medicina." *Boletín de Psicología* 4(3):1–10.

Zimbalist, A. 1987. "Editor's Introduction: Cuba's Socialist Economy Toward the 1990s." *World Development* 15(1):1–4.

———. 1992. "Teetering on the Brink: Cuba's Current Economic and Political Crisis." *Journal of Latin American Studies* 24:407–18.

Zimbalist, A., ed. 1988. *Cuban Political Economy.* Boulder, Colo.: Westview.

Zimbalist, A., and C. Brundenius. 1989. *The Cuban Economy: Measurement and Analysis of Socialist Performance.* Baltimore, Md.: Johns Hopkins University Press.

Zimbalist, A., and S. Eckstein. 1987. "Patterns of Cuban Development: The First Twenty-five Years." *World Development* 15(1):5–22.

Index